SMART IS THE NEW RICH,

...AND SMART RETIREES C.H.E.A.T.

(CREATE HIGHLY EFFECTIVE ALTERNATIVE TECHNIQUES)

Smart Is The New Rich,
...and Smart Retirees C.H.E.A.T.
(Create Highly Effective Alternative Techniques)

The following phrases are federally registered trademarks:

- Don't just manage your money, master your money®
- Insure your income, insure your outcomes, invest the rest with purpose®
- Security is Sexy®
- IQ Wealth Management®

Steve Jurich and IQ Wealth Management
7702 E. Doubletree Ranch Road, Suite 300,
Scottsdale, AZ 85258

Printed in the United States of America
First Printing 2013
Second Edition 2019

10 9 8 7 6 5 4 3 2 1

ISBN
9780989053891

Library of Congress
Control Number:

DEDICATION

Dedicated to my sweet mom...A Partisan soldier and one of the greatest leaders of all time.
... And a heck of a coach.

DISCLAIMER

TABLE OF CONTENTS

TABLE OF CONTENTS

P O P   Q U I Z . . .

We all want it. Most of us feel we don't have enough of it. Those who do have enough, usually want more. What is it?

Financial independence, otherwise known as "wealth."

That often elusive but sometimes overpowering goal that keeps the world getting up in the morning.

Wealth is defined differently by each person. For some, it is the attainment of an actual numerical goal in terms of dollars and possessions. To others, it is the knowledge that you have provided for loved ones, paid all debts and made good on your promises. Still others measure their progress by their ability to help the less fortunate or their church. A simplified definition might be: "No more money worries, no matter what." Regardless, getting there and staying there requires a fully integrated financial plan in this "new normal" of puny interest rates, unpredictable markets, and political strife.

The key questions: "how much money do I need to save in order to retire, and how do I invest my money so that I will never run out of income?" Your answers to those two questions determine your financial fate. This book will help you with that.

> *"'How could I have been such an idiot?'*
>
> *If you've never yelled out that sentence at yoursel in a fury,*
>
> *you're not an investor."*
>
> **-Jason Zweig, author of Your Money & Your Brain, editor- The Intelligent Investor, Wall Street Journal**

As a Retirement Coach, it's my goal to get you to a position of permanent wealth and financial peace with a feeling of certainty about your finances. You want the inner sense that you are going to get where you want to go in this world for as many years as you have on this planet, based on contractual guarantees combined with mathematically sound investing.

My plan for you is not based on market "Rules of Thumb," or the "13 Things You Need to Do with Your Money Now." It is based on nearly two decades of working with real investors in retirement mode—either in retirement or just before arriving. My typical clients hold portfolios in the six, seven and eight figure ranges.

These are smart people. They are achievers in their careers. Many are engineers, teachers, business owners, managers and technicians. They include physicians, dentists, chiropractors and state government workers. They didn't need me when they were growing their money. They either handled their own investments or hired accumulation specialists who placed 100 percent of their professional focus on building piles of cash. I help people build and preserve mountains of cash, but because my focus is on helping people retire, I work also in the area of building rivers of cash flow, and making sure the right people end up with your money in the right amounts at the right time. I focus on retirement income planning as the beginning step in building a comprehensive retirement plan. Why? Very simply, there is no retirement without income. You don't want an "on again, off again" plan or a hope-so plan. You want a *know-so* plan.

But here's the problem: at least 95 percent of the information you can find about how to invest your hard-earned money is focused on aggressively accumulating dollars for a retirement that is still at least 10 to 20 years away. My clients are retired right now, or will be in the next five years.

As Founder of IQ Wealth Management and host of the *MASTERING MONEY* show on Money Radio, my priority is creating more informed consumers who understand their entire range of options.

It's been said that "knowledge is power," and it is my belief that knowledge—properly applied--can lead to an attainable destination for you: Lasting Wealth.

Which Brings Us To The IQ Wealth Smarter Bucketing System™

Relax! Enjoy life. Retire and STAY retired! Stop micromanaging pennies and start collecting spendable dollars with the IQ Wealth Smarter Bucketing Retirement System™. Learn why playing the game like a good "doobie" according to the old rules will almost ensure you fall short of your goals in retirement.

Instead, learn the secret to permanent financial success and reliable cash flow. Learn how you, too, can C.H.E.A.T. (Create Highly Effective Alternative Techniques) to win. In fact, you may be crazy if you don't start C.H.E.A.T.I.N.G soon!

The IQ Wealth Smarter Bucketing System™ is a Specific, Measurable, Attainable, Reliable and Timely path to a "You-Proof" Retirement. The plan is based on L.U.C.K. (Liquidity, Utility, Control, Knowledge.)

Now you can avoid making D.U.M.B. money mistakes (Diversifying Under Misguided Beliefs). Here's the good news: Managed correctly, maybe your retirement "Number" need not be as big as you once thought. You're about to learn how to take your "Number," go forth, prosper, and sustain a lifestyle. When you start enjoying more sustainable income with fewer dollars, regardless of the markets, you'll understand why more people are saying:

Insure your income, insure your outcomes, invest the rest with purpose®, because

Smart IS The New Rich.

ABOUT THE AUTHOR

STEVE JURICH

- Retirement Coach
- Wealth Manager
- Radio Personality
- Founder of IQ Wealth Management®
- Kiplinger® Contributor

Retirement Coach Steve Jurich Says

"Smart Is The New Rich" When It Comes To Building Lasting Income"

The following is a press release appearing on TheStreet.com and MarketWatch.com, based on an interview by the Celebrity Press Agency

About the Author: Steve Jurich, Retirement Coach and Founder of IQ Wealth Management, a registered investment adviser, speaks more like a favorite professor than an insurance agent, or even a retirement adviser. Unlike the breed of annuity agents who use pressure tactics and tired lures like "free steak dinners" to gain captive audiences, Jurich's priority is creating more informed consumers. He takes time to make sure his clients understand the range of options available to retirees so they become better educated investors on the whole. That investment of time is a significant one for Jurich (pronounced "Jur-itch"), but he believes the results his clients see in their portfolios speak for themselves. It's been said that "knowledge is power," and when that knowledge is applied wisely, Jurich believes it can lead to a desirable destination: lasting wealth.

The amount of conflicting and ever-changing information in the media combined with market volatility and outright fear-mongering has made reliable information on wealth management a rare and valuable commodity. Annuities in particular have come through the media gauntlet battered - at a time when the right annuity might be the best foundation for ensuring lasting income during retirement.

As pensions have become a thing of the past in America, many investors are discovering or re-discovering the benefits of annuities. According to Jurich, annuities are the only regulated financial instrument that can contractually guarantee a lifetime income, and can help save retirees from investment mistakes that could result in income shortfall at the most critical time in their lives.

Yet journalists from *Marketwatch*, *Smart Money*, and the *Wall Street Journal* have portrayed annuity sales people as all but twisting the ends of their mustaches while tying retirees' savings to railroad tracks. *Smart Money's* article "Ten Things Your Variable-Annuity Seller Won't Tell You," quotes an insurance salesman referring to commission as the key reason for selling them. Obviously, every financial product comes with a production and delivery cost. Compensation for competent professional assistance also has a value. In truth, the compensation on fixed index annuities is far less than the long term costs of many mutual fund portfolios, whose fees never disappear. "It's important to note that compensation on index annuities for the advisor does not reduce the value of the owner's account. No deduction is made and the client does not pay an advisory fee. This is a system of compensation for professional service that is economical." Jurich agrees that variable annuities, with continuous fee deductions and sequence of returns risk, may not be the right fit for truly moderate and conservative investors. Because the compensation for the agent on hybrids does not reduce the account value "One hundred percent of my clients' assets go to work on day one without reduction by fees."

Still, the journalistic attack is relentless. When a popular television financial whiz like Suze Orman declares on CNN Money "I hate variable annuities" - and then shrilly repeats that sentence three more times with increasingly wider grimaces, you know you've hit upon a controversial subject. The danger is that it's too easy for those unfamiliar with annuities to lump them altogether, as in the Kiplinger article, titled "The Great Annuity Rip-Off," in which the writer calls out "unscrupulous agents" who manipulate seniors into overpriced, risky investments.

Jurich says, "I'm always amazed by journalists who place themselves higher on the rung of research knowledge than the Wharton School of Business, Harvard, Stanford, The University of Illinois, Boston University, Boston College, and the U.S. Government Accounting and Budget Office. They've spent years doing actual research studying the subject, not just a few hours on Google™. All of these institutions promote the effectiveness of annuities as being part of the solution rather than the problem in securing dependable and sustainable lifetime income."

Today's retirees have had enough of self-serving and out of date advisors who still sell the same ideas that worked in the Bull markets of the 1980's and 1990's. Instead of seeking professional advice, 50 percent of middle-income retirees choose to turn to the internet for guidance on retirement planning – and 38 percent would rather ask family or friends than a professional, according to a study released by the Bankers Life and Casualty Company Center for a Secure Retirement. Jurich doesn't blame investors for looking to other resources. Because of the poor experiences they may have had with advisors in the past and so many publicized corporate misdeeds, trust is the rarest of all commodities.

Finding a trusted advisor is more difficult than ever. A key reason is that the consumer can't always be certain about just who the advisor is working for. Stock brokers work for a broker dealer. Insurance agents represent the insurance company. Advisers who pass the Series 65 exam are licensed as fiduciaries, meaning they are required to act in the client's best interest. Jurich takes his responsibility as an advisor very seriously. It is an important difference that consumers are wise to consider. In fact, he says there are three types of annuity agents whom retirees have seen all too often. He strives to be the fourth kind.

"There's the agent who believes he's doing a good job, but hasn't done enough research to give full financial advice, and might not even have a securities license – an insurance-only agent shouldn't look at your securities portfolio. Then there's the agent who understands how annuities work, but cares more about commissions and sales awards. They're not willing to take the time to compare the best companies and payouts for you," he says. The third type of agent is frequently seen in brokerage firms, and is the most dangerous to retirement funds –one that Jurich describes as "the agent whose cheese has been moved." This agent thrived in the good old days, says Jurich, when variable annuities and REITS were the greatest things to hit investors since the rise of tech companies. "They're well-spoken, articulate, even funny, but have done little or no research on the new annuity options, which doesn't stop them from giving you their opinions on them. What they're saying is 'I hope you buy a variable annuity instead of the hybrid one that I don't completely understand,'" he says. "Annuities are not accumulation vehicles. At their best they are income and preservation vehicles. The new buzzword is 'decumulation.' That's their wheelhouse."

Besides his role as a Wealth Manager (www.IQWealth.com), Jurich is a leading expert on Next Generation Hybrid Index Annuities and manages several dividend portfolios. He believes in a bucketing strategy that incorporates annuities for lifetime income and preservation in one bucket, alongside a dividend reinvestment bucket.

He is the Editor-in-Chief of MyAnnuityGuy.com, and host of the popular radio show, MASTERING MONEY, on Money Radio. In fact, he's a little like the Hybrid Annuities he favors – a strong blend of virtues. He acknowledges that while retirees want the secure income fixed annuities may provide, they're rightly wary of the hard sell, hidden fees, penalties and surrender charges. "Annuities are part investment, part insurance. Used properly, there's no reason to pay a surrender charge. There can be ample liquidity options."

Part of Jurich's work is to educate retirees on all their annuity options, both strengths and weaknesses. "Annuities are only one piece of the puzzle, but a piece that can no longer be ignored. Immediate annuities in magazines look good in the ad, until you learn your money is gone if you die– that's not acceptable for most people," says Jurich.

One of the main concerns keeping retirees up at night is the dilemma of choosing between risk investments that can turn south or interest rates that don't even match inflation. While immediate annuities can promise as much as a 9.56 percent income payout, the problem is this: "If you put your life savings into that and die early, your money is gone," says Jurich. Another option is a Joint Immediate Annuity, which reduces income to 6.2 percent, but continues if there is one surviving spouse. If both spouses die, however, the heirs are left with the same problem – the money tied up in that annuity is gone. Then along came hybrid annuities with advanced income riders, blending the virtues of the immediate annuity, the sense of safety found in old fashioned bonds, that "allow you to be a little bit pregnant or a little bit married" to the lifetime income. Modern income riders on fixed index annuities can create a pensionized lifetime income stream, without the irrevocability of the immediate annuity.

The fixed annuity is one of the central branches near the trunk of the annuity tree. It acts similar to a savings account at a bank. It can be used to save capital, and is accessible via penalty free withdrawals within limits. It accrues interest, tax deferred like an IRA. Safety, security, and the option of lifelong income are the selling points. Still, with interest rates so low, variable annuities have appeal.

Five years ago, variable annuities offered what appeared to be attractive programs: "They would guarantee whatever the stock market did on the upside, or 7 percent, whichever was higher," says Jurich. "But this was a play on words for some agents." Jurich is quick to point out that the so called "7" percent was misunderstood by many and possibly misrepresented by many.

"Some consumers wrongly assumed they were earning 7% on their money--or the gains of the market whichever was better. False. Variable annuities place the principal investment risk on the investor, which is why they are sold via prospectus under securities law, outlining risks and fees." (Conversely, Next Generation hybrid index annuities are built on a fixed annuity chassis, whose interest is linked to upward market movements. They are not securities driven, but rather savings vehicles.) "With a variable annuity, your return is based on the performance of the mutual funds within the variable annuity, known as 'sub accounts.'" Jurich continues, " Here's where the danger starts for many investors. The 7%, or 6% or 5% you hear about is a mathematical income base from which to calculate a lifetime income stream guaranteed by the life insurance company. It is not a guarantee of your principal or in any way a guarantee of a return on that principal. In fact, the income base is not even money. It is a slide rule income calculator. The typical variable annuity has an a la carte menu of fees that can buy benefits and guarantees. You get what you pay for, but you keep paying. I don't want to be overly harsh on variable annuities. The fees actually do buy benefits, and the benefits can be very useful. The key for the consumer is understanding what they are buying, and making sure the feature applies to their situation. I think you get in trouble when you view an annuity as investment. It is more of a financial appliance. You can add a lot of bells and whistles to stoves and refrigerators, some you may not need."

Jurich points out that the sub accounts provide the fee base for the insurance carrier on a variable annuity. Unlike fixed and hybrid annuities, when the account values drop across the board on a trillion dollars worth of assets, the general fee revenue of the variable annuity industry gets decimated. "The insurance company, when it did its math to give the '7%', assumed the stock market would perform at a range of 6% to 12%. The other assumption was that treasuries would keep paying 5% to 6%. Woops. 'Shift' happens."

According to Jurich, what makes Next Generation Hybrid Index Annuities a different breed from the rest is a calibrated blend of interest earnings linked to upward movements of market indexes, combined with a base of mathematically assured income. "Inexperienced agents try to sell them as stock market alternatives. They are not. Hybrid annuities are more akin to the bond component in a portfolio. They bring more to the table, however, that bonds can't begin to touch: an actuarially sound pensionized income that can be turned on or turned off at will. In a turbulent world like we now face, the protection of principal values cannot be overlooked" he says. Listening to Jurich, one senses that Hybrid annuities may be either a missing link, or part of the next phase in the evolution of income planning.

"No matter how aggressive you are, you still have to manage your risks. Skilled investors and traders don't gamble all their money. They stack their winnings, reduce losses, and play with the house's money. An annuity strategy protects you from your own worst enemy: You. One part of your portfolio should be protected against market risk, interest rate risk, and systematic risk. You need a truly non-correlated income holding to offset the risks you are taking in other parts of your portfolio; Not something that zigs or zags, but rather sits still when turmoil arises. A rock. You can spend years searching for the "ideal" investment, but the time you lose could be costly. The Hybrid annuity is like a durable luxury car built on a rugged SUV chassis, ready for you to turn the key." Unlike variable annuities, there are no annual fees for management. In fact there are no upfront or annual fees except for the income or death benefit riders, which Jurich is highly in favor of.

"Underneath every annuity is an immediate annuity waiting to happen. If you preserve your principal with a deferred annuity, you retain the ability to "annuitize" at a later date when your payout will be so much higher. Annuitizing may be premature at younger ages prior to age 65, 70, or 75." Jurich says. That's where income riders solve the problem by providing a 'lighter version' of annuitizing, but with all the heavy artillery to back them up. The Guaranteed Lifetime Income Rider (GLIR) has revolutionized income planning. The Hybrid earns acceptable indexed interest, while not being actually in the market. Under the microscope, the yields are bond-like, not equity-like, which is fine. Especially when actual investment grade bonds are paying microscopic interest and the dividends on the S & P are only around 2%. Annuity critics forget that most retirees want a floor under their money."

Jurich advises that one shouldn't expect to hit home runs with an index annuity, just as you wouldn't expect a bond portfolio to double overnight. Purpose dictates placement. "Preservation matters," he says. "Preservation has value. If you can simultaneously preserve value while building future income benefits similar to a pension, that's a home run today. Joe Di Maggio has passed away, Mrs. Robinson. We aren't living in an era of spectacular gains. The goal is to avoid spectacular losses, keep money flowing in, and do the things you want to do while you have time—preferably with your shirt on." Jurich explains, "One part of your portfolio needs to be a rock. When it can build akin to a pension at work, when you can turn the income on and off at will, and when you can lay your head on your pillow at night knowing your money will be there when you wake up in the morning,—fully intact—this may become your most prized possession."

But what happens to your money if the worst should happen to you? "I don't necessarily like 98% of Hybrid annuities. The 2% I do like waive surrender charges upon death, allowing spouses and children to inherit without paying to get the money out. But let's say there's a medical emergency requiring long term, or at-home care. You can build in "Assisted Care" payouts to provide extra income to help pay for long term care costs. It's that kind of flexibility, in addition to protection from losses plus sustainable income that completes the package. Jurich calls it a "SWAN" strategy, an acronym for "Sleep Well At Night."

But this all probably sounds like the sales pitch we've heard about variable and lifetime annuities. Jurich is very frank when he lays out the most common concerns: "Retirees are worried about the loss of control that came with older style annuities. Specifically, they were concerned about the inability to take out money without paying penalties, about the inability to change the income stream, and about the possibility that when they died, the insurance company might keep the remaining value of their annuity." "The new generation of Next Generation Hybrid Index Annuities addresses these concerns," says Jurich.

Fact: The Annuities Of Old Are A Thing Of The Past™

Jurich sees the new forms of Next Generation index annuities in a new light: not as strictly accumulation vehicles but as power tools for income and preservation in a balanced portfolio. Although not officially an asset class, the case is strong. Here is an asset that can provide preservation and income, sitting outside the typical pie chart of stock and bond mutual funds and ETFs. There are no market losses, ever. Your money can only go up, never down, forward never back in relation to a market index. Your money is never directly invested in the market. It is guarded and protected by established, audited, regulated insurance companies—many of which are more than a hundred years old and have never lost a penny for any annuity owner. If you are safety minded, explore these new annuities.

Security of principal matters in retirement. Meanwhile your income can grow at a rate of 6% to 8% every year you delay income, much like Social Security. Your rate of income for life can be 5% to 9% depending on your age and deferral period, with your principal never at risk to the market. Talk about peace of mind! Next Generation Hybrid Index Annuities can provide resistance to interest rate risk. They protect against longevity risk in the way that immediate annuities can with a key difference: Using a guaranteed lifetime income rider (GLIR), a retiree can avoid the irreversible decision of the immediate annuity.

Asked what he views as a key reason to consider Hybrid annuities as part of a well planned retirement, he answers: "Who can afford the loss of fifty percent of their life savings anymore? It happened in 2000 and again in 2008. You may see two or three more "once-in-a-lifetime" crashes in your lifetime. Why not protect yourself? He refers to the new generation of Next Generation Hybrid Index Annuities as "Luxury Hybrids", providing true diversification to stocks, along with a secure income foundation for life. Income will determine your retirement future. Running out of money is unacceptable. The right annuity can provide income that can last two lifetimes – yours, and your spouse's." It's that search for stability that has driven the demand for annuities as primary alternatives for IRA, 401k, and 403b rollovers, including Roth rollovers. Jurich says "The Baby Boomer generation cannot withstand another 2008." He summarizes: "Insure your income, insure your outcomes, invest the rest with purpose. The IQ Wealth Smarter Bucketing Retirement System™ can keep you on track, make life more simple, and help you to stop worrying. Finally, you can retire and stay retired."

As Steve likes to say "Don't just manage your money, MASTER your money."®

WEBSITES:

www.IQWealthManagement.com www.MyAnnuityGuy.com

WALL STREET AND MAIN STREET

- It's said on Wall Street that when a man with money meets a man with experience, the man with experience ends up with money and the man with money ends up with experience...

- Over on Main Street it's said that an ounce of prevention is worth a pound of cure. They're both right.

- Conclusion: You're no longer in a race to die with the most toys, you're in a fight to live the way you've always dreamed. Let's do this.

CHAPTER 1

KEEPING IT SIMPLE ISN'T STUPID...
WELCOME TO THE NEW NORMAL

ONCE UPON A TIME, A MILLION DOLLARS in a 401(k) and a free-and-clear home meant your money worries were over. You could retire, turn on your pension, collect $60,000 a year in interest, and still pass on a million to your loved ones.

That was then; this is now.

Today, after the "dot-com" crash, 9-11 and the 2008 "Black Swan," Americans are not sure where they stand. Is Wall Street on their side? Or is it a rigged game? As 78 million Baby Boomers march into retirement at a pace of 10,000 per day, they aren't worrying about the same things anymore. A recent MetLife study, confirmed by Cerulli Associates of Boston, found that the number-one fear of retiring Americans is no longer dying – it's running out of money.

It wasn't too long ago that Frank, a prospective client, walked into my office looking kind of miffed and depressed. At first, I couldn't understand why. He seemed to be a bright man in pretty good health, and, as it turned out, he was sitting on a portfolio of roughly a million dollars and change. "What could be bad?" you may be wondering.

He had worked as an engineer for a major Fortune 500 company and owned both company stock and a 401(k) that he had rolled over into an IRA. He was a 68-year-old happily married guy with three grown kids and two grandkids who had taken early retirement at age 58. His dad had passed away, but his mom was still alive at age 90. We shook hands, exchanged pleasantries, and sat down at my desk. The sunlight shone in a little bright at that time of the day, so I skewed the blinds and asked how I could be of help.

"I just can't seem to get a handle on it," he said, with a facial expression that I could only read as fatigue. "When I had my 401(k) in the '80s and '90s, it seemed I could do no wrong. I picked a lot of different kinds of sector funds and almost all of them seemed to go up. If they fell, I would switch funds and still see nice gains. My bond funds were my best investment until about five or six years ago. I figured one day, they would be my retirement. Now, they're all losing money. I spent an hour a day on Morningstar and Yahoo, studying different fund managers and philosophies. I contributed the max every year to my 401(k). Honestly, it was kind of fun, and I felt pretty confident about my grip on the markets. Before I knew it, I was sitting on a million and then the statements went up to over $1.6 million before I finally retired. Then came the dot-com bubble." I could see a microcosm of joy turned into frustration in his eyes— telling a story I've heard before from people like Frank.

It turned out, we were just getting warmed up. I encouraged him to continue and listened intently as he opened a meticulously organized book of monthly financial statements going back 12 months. Frank, I perceived, was an orderly person who enjoyed some risk, but also required symmetry and a level of precision in his affairs. His investments weren't cooperating.

He continued. "Since then, I've hired the best advisors money can buy—big name brokers--and have never really recovered. In fact, according to the plan my advisor created for me back in 1999, I should be sitting on somewhere between $2.4 million and $3.5 million right now, sipping margaritas. Hell, I never thought it was going to be like this. The guy I hired was a pretty sharp CFP with a big company logo standing behind him. I felt like I had stepped up to the big leagues, and was on cloud nine for a while. I was impressed with the level of research on each stock that I asked about, and I enjoyed seeing projections of my portfolio values into the future. The plan was nice, neat, and colorful. Everything was crisp, just like I like it. Besides, I liked the guy. The stocks were all names I heard in the press daily. They seemed fine. I really didn't know how to analyze each stock. I guess looking back, I didn't know exactly why I owned each stock. I couldn't tell you my exact strategy, but it looked to be what other smart people must be doing, so I went with it. I had asked him about dividend investing, but he said that he could do better with "pure growth and momentum stocks." A friend of mine had done really well by reinvesting dividends, and I still wonder if I would have been better off in a dividend reinvestment portfolio.

He wasn't well versed with annuities. The annuities he offered were variable annuities, which seemed quite expensive, or immediate annuities which would force me to lose control of my principal to the insurance company. Neither seemed very appealing. He mentioned long term care insurance which struck a cord, but we never did anything about it. Seeing my dad develop dementia had me wondering if I needed some form of insurance. Most of all, he showed me a Monte Carlo simulation of a thousand possible outcomes for my investments and eventual income withdrawals. No one had ever done that for me before."

His brow started to clear. It became obvious that Frank was a math guy with a flair for speculation. He liked to see spreadsheets and really didn't like the idea of guessing about things that were important to his future plans. The Monte Carlo simulations added a sense of science being applied to calculated risk projections. The calculations justified some of the risk he was taking. From an investor profile perspective, Frank could be described as a combination of a Family Steward, which comprise about 20.7 percent of high net worth investors according to studies, and an Independent, which comprise approximately 12.9 percent of higher net worth investors. It's a fairly common pairing actually.

To the Family Steward, taking care of family and making wise financial decisions go hand in hand. Their personal senses of worth and self-images are tied to how well they manage their nest eggs. They aren't just thinking of themselves when they make their carefully thought-out decisions; they feel they are making them for their spouses, kids, parents, and even the U.S. economy. They supported their kids' high school projects and may tithe regularly at church if they are church goers; however, it is not a requirement of a Family Steward to go to church—it's just inbred.

The Independent is the person who enjoys investing and is optimistic that their decisions today will lead to a better life tomorrow. They have confidence in themselves, bordering on overconfidence at times. They don't mind taking advice from a source they truly put on a pedestal; otherwise, get out of their way—they can do it themselves. In most areas of life, especially at work, this trait helps them to succeed. In the investment world, the irrationality of markets simply doesn't make sense to them (as if it ever could!). The Independent can be his or her own best friend, or worst enemy, depending on the circumstances. To the Independent, successful investing creates a sense of personal freedom. They regard investing

SMART IS THE NEW RICH

as a means to a greater end and believe that simply knowing more statistics should lead to greater success. To them, retiring early is the evidence—the scoreboard--of how well they handled their money. They won't admit to being competitive about their "number" (their net worth) and wondering how other investors are doing. But it drives them crazy, if they let it.

Frank's self-esteem was heading for a crisis--he was beginning to feel like *he was a failure*, not his plan

"Frankly, looking back, the only lines on the Monte Carlo that got my attention were the ones leading toward the $3 million range and above. I've never considered failure as an option. The spreadsheets we're impressive also. They showed me going all the way to age 85. It looked like a $7 million net worth, taking $50,000 a year from investments was not unrealistic at all. I confirmed it on the internet with several other calculators. Everything on the internet and in the money magazines said the moderate range of 10 percent to 12.8 percent was reasonable. Bonds were always paying 6 percent to 7 percent, so Plan B, if things got drastic, was always there."

"The financial plan I paid for was pretty intricate. I was told I could withdraw 5 percent a year safely back then, which turned out to be poor advice, but I don't hold a grudge—I believed it myself. My funds took a hit in '01 and '02, and I started taking income at the same time. The statements kept going down by thousands every month and really started to dwindle, so I cut back and even postponed a trip my wife and I had planned. My wife was getting upset and it even was affecting our relationship. It wasn't supposed to be like this. I went to a couple of investment dinner seminars and the people giving the presentations seemed to be pretty sharp. They all seemed

5 | P A G E

to be pointing to the same thing: variable annuities and managed accounts. I went with one of the advisors. She recommended a natural gas partnership, a REIT, and some TICs (Tenant In Common Real Estate Investments). Those haven't done so well. In fact, I have to put money into the TICs to keep them afloat. I have a number of stocks and a REIT that are just sitting there doing nothing. I can't sell them; I can't really do anything with them. It is just lost money in my view."

I asked Frank who was managing his money currently.

"Been doing it myself for four years, and I'm not doing much better, but at least I don't have to pay someone for poor results."

Frank found that good information is available everywhere, but applied knowledge is the real key to lasting success.

We were half way through our meeting, as Frank began to summarize, "Honestly, the prospect of making only 8 percent or so was off my radar. I would have considered it failing. I truly believed the 12 percent to 16 percent range was where everything was heading and was not at all unrealistic." (A Gallup poll from 1999 confirms Frank's thesis. Today, I would take 8 percent and kiss the advisor that could give it to me, man or woman!) "Looking back now," Frank said, "I can say that the real reason I had chosen that company and that CFP I was because I thought they knew things about the market that I didn't. My sense was that I could make 10 percent to 12 percent on my own—I had done it already. I wanted to move up. With the help of a serious professional with a serious research department, I thought I could move my results to the next level. Secretly, I was expecting 16 percent. We both said out loud that it was a bit of a reach, but not totally unrealistic, and even had a little laugh about it. After all, the markets had averaged an 18.5 percent return since 1983—we were being realists; not expecting to ride a gravy train."

As exaggerated as Frank's confession might sound, I can assure you that it reflects common beliefs at the time. Frank is only one of many.

Frank continued, "This was late 1998, so in retrospect, I would have to admit that I pretty much got used to the 20 percent and 30 percent returns. They felt good. I felt good. Down deep, I knew it couldn't last, but the market just kept going up. Who was I to argue with it? Besides, the research I was doing, the research from the brokerage, and the Monte Carlo simulator all just seemed to confirm what I believed. It was flashing green for me."

I use Monte Carlo simulation in my practice and it is a valuable tool, but it is only a source of information, not applied knowledge. It is a map of the territory, but as the saying goes, the map is *not* the territory. Life and markets are what happens when you're making other plans.

We continued to talk as he encouraged me to look through his holdings. His statement was at least nine pages. He had page after page, double sided, of mutual funds and ETFs that I recognized as overlapping. I searched for a trend in his investment strategy, hoping to find a pattern. None was apparent. He had at least 70 different holdings on his statements, mixed between stock and bond funds and ETFs.

I began to ask him why he owned some of them. Each item had its own justification. He felt like he was not being haphazard at all. In fact, he told a compelling story on almost every one.

The recurring theme was an article he read, or a newsletter guru offering special reports with the "5 Can't Miss Stocks," etc. He was a fan of both CNBC and Fox and bought favorite picks he heard about on those shows. I noticed several buy and sell entries for the SPY ETF. Clearly, he was floundering. Was he investing, or trading?

His portfolio reminded me of a lady my mom used to know who bet on every horse at each horse race. My mom was a hard-working realtor and entrepreneur who would never risk a dime in stocks, but took plenty of flyers on vacant land, and some panned out nicely. She also loved Las Vegas and the horse track, but never gambled more than a few hundred dollars. She actually was practicing good asset allocation without knowing it—bucketing most of her money into safe assets, investing in what she understood (real estate), and saving pure speculation for Las Vegas, rather than her income money. Her friend was a systems thinker who apparently believed in diversification. Why bet on one horse when you can bet on 'em all? True, she had a winner in every race, but she soon learned the cost of broad diversification is a very low return, and that the odds are not in favor of the amateur better. Both the stock market and the track are zero sum games. All the money will be paid out after the house takes its cut. In both arenas, Pareto's Law applies: 20 percent of participants make 80 percent of the gains, while 80 percent of participants must live with the remaining 20 percent. It seems to work in all areas of life, actually.

The lesson that Frank was learning--with hard won dollars-- is the lesson of Secular Bear and Bull Markets mixed in with a little of Pareto's Law. Bubbles have a way of skewing Pareto's Law, for a while. All markets move in cycles and the numbers eventually right themselves. There are small cycles with short durations of a month to a year that are like a storm that can be handled with a raincoat and an umbrella. And then there are large cycles that are very powerful, based on dynamic forces of supply and demand that can last from 10 to 20 years. These are more like long-term hurricanes. I recommend staying out of their paths. The Fed might have you thinking that we are in a new Bull phase, but real analysis says we are in a shorter cyclical Bull market within a long term secular bear. Stay on the right side of regression to the mean, and the right side of history.

Is Frank's story out of the ordinary? Not according to Gallup Polls

On April 20, 2011 Gallup's headline read: "In U.S., 54% Have Stock Market Investments, Lowest Since 1999." The average American did not necessarily own stocks in the 1960s or 1970s. Stock market participation increased dramatically in the 1980s and steadily progressed and hit full bloom in 2002, the worst year of the Millennial Crash, when 67 percent of Americans owned stock in some form.

Moreover, Frank is a member of the six figure income club, meaning that he had a nearly 90 percent chance of considering the stock market a safe place for money, and the best long term investment. Gallup reported that "Eighty-seven percent of upper-income Americans -- those making $75,000 or more annually -- own stocks, as do 83 percent of postgraduates and 73 percent of college graduates. Sixty-four percent of Republicans hold stocks, compared with half of Democrats and independents. Men are more likely than women to be stock owners. Those aged 50 to 64 are the most likely of any age group to say they have money invested in the stock market."

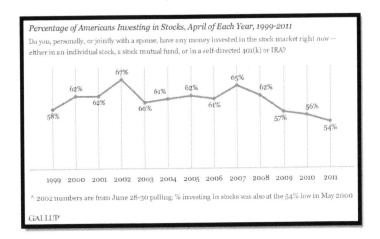

Percentage of Americans Investing in Stocks, April of Each Year, 1999-2011

Do you, personally, or jointly with a spouse, have any money invested in the stock market right now -- either in an individual stock, a stock mutual fund, or in a self-directed 401(k) or IRA?

^ 2002 numbers are from June 28-30 polling; % investing in stocks was also at the 54% low in May 2000

GALLUP

According to polls, Frank was suffering from a case of the "normals"

Frank was clearly not out of the ordinary; in fact, he was part of the mainstream. Go back and view the literature of the times. If you go back to 1999, investors had a love affair with the stock market. Warren Buffett explained at the Allen and Co. gathering in Sun Valley, Idaho that year that the Fortune 500 index of common stocks was trading at 30 times earnings and was dooming U.S. large caps to 17 years of sub-par performance. Stocks had performed spectacularly from August of 1982 to that summer day in 1999. After 17 years of only occasional and mostly mild market corrections and years of prosperity, common stock investors were in love with stocks. There was no telling them otherwise. Paraphrasing Buffett, "Picking common stocks was the national pastime."

Frank is an intelligent man, and he was steeped in research from the internet. He read the investment books, magazines, charts, and graphs. His decisions were all rational in his mind.

As good as his information seemed, as many times as he corroborated the story and confirmed his calculations, he was still dealing with an imperfect knowledge of future outcomes, using imperfect financial tools, taking on an imperfect system known as the market. The real problem is that he was trying to do all of that with finite time and finite resources. Not a good combination for Frank.

Frank's New Challenge Was Not Trying To Make His Accounts Grow—It Was Trying To Secure More Income With Fewer Dollars and Keep The Market From Eating His Money.

Frank and I moved our discussion from his current investments to the real reason he had come to see me: Income. His plan had always been built around accumulation. Strategies for income and strategies for accumulation are radically opposed. The math is completely different.

De-cumulation is an opposite science and discipline from A-ccumulation. (Pardon my hyphens)

His game plan had broken down. He was in plan 'B' territory, but kept trying to get to his destination with a faulty Plan 'A'.

Frank's long-held and well-considered strategy was to invest very aggressively through about age 54, then get a little more moderate through retirement age at 58, and then put at least half his money into bonds earning 6 percent or 7 percent at some point.

His next words shocked me:

"Ten years ago, if you had talked to me about an annuity, I would have figured you were a full-fledged member of the Flat Earth Society. Five years ago, if you mentioned it, I still might have laughed, but not quite as hard. Today, I'm suddenly looking to sign up. Is it me, or is it everybody?"

When It Comes To Your Investments, Are You Still Fighting The Last War?

Recall the 1980s and 1990s when Baby Boomers in their 30s, 40s and 50s poured money into their 401(k)s with every paycheck, driving the demand for stocks. They created a long, slow hurricane.

Those same 78 million Baby Boomers are now in their 50s, 60s, and 70s--and naturally scaling back on risk and consumption. Rather than pouring money into the markets with every paycheck – they're taking money out to replace their paychecks. The hurricane has reversed. And it might also be long and slow.

This isn't a minor blip on the screen; it is a major reversal of a mega-trend. Fighting a new high-tech war with conventional weapons may result in heavy casualties. Any investor expecting the same results with pie chart investments that worked in a different era is asking for the law of supply and demand to be repealed. This is a seismic demographic shift and one that is making its way to both Wall Street and Wal-Mart. Wall *Street* is feeling the pinch. Wal-*Mart* is opening 24 hour mega-plexes.

If the slowdown and reversal affected just the Baby Boomers, that would be powerful enough. But realize that the Silent Generation, also called the Lucky Few who grew up in the 1930s and 1940s are still kicking and going strong. They were part of the tidal wave of innovation and investing that turned the 1980s into the biggest innovation and monetary expansion in the history of capitalism. It isn't just their population that matters; it's their system of buying behaviors.

When younger, Baby Boomers drove the markets and drove big SUVs to fancy malls. Now they're downshifting, driving smaller hybrid

SUVs, and driving past the malls. They're staying on the job longer and taking a few jobs from Generations X and Y. The younger generations, who should be our hope for sustained growth, are suffering from 25 percent underemployment. They're not stuffing money into Wall Street's coffers for several reasons: A) They don't have the money; B) They don't trust Wall Street - or the economy for that matter. And, they don't believe social security will be there for them in any form. They may carry a fresh memory of their parents' stock market accounts getting crushed twice and maybe even saw mom and dad's house go into short-sale. These generations are going to wait to see how things go. To many of them, Apple is the stock market, which means they are repeating the same mistakes their parents made.

Along with the rest of the country, Frank was realizing that the market is not always a profit machine. From age 25 to 55, you are in the Accumulation and Contribution Phase. Once you cross the 55 mark, you enter a more moderate phase where the plan should be to start moving to preservation in order to preserve your position. On the day you retire and officially stop receiving a pay check, you enter a new phase which financial planners call the "De-cumulation Phase." This is a 50-dollar word which simply means that you are no longer contributing and growing your money - you are living off of it.

Key Math Principle:

In retirement, your withdrawals replace your contributions. The same compounding effect that can make you rich in the accumulation phase can make you poor in the "de-cumulation" phase.

It is known as "reverse compounding", and is the enemy of any

retirement portfolio. Unfortunately, it is overlooked by most investors.

This book is dedicated to helping you combat the problem.

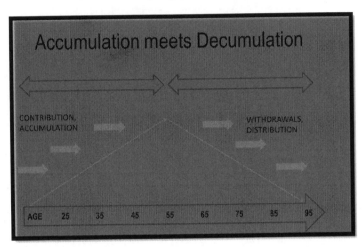

<u>The measure of intelligence is not the amount of money in your account; it is the act of adapting to changes in a timely manner.</u>

If you are frustrated like Frank, go easy on yourself. Not only are you entering a *new normal* like the rest of the world, you are entering one that is custom-made for you, based on your age and circumstances.

I could just say, "man up," but I know how hard it can be to change and I have seen many intelligent people wrestle with the idea of knowing it's time to get more conservative. Getting more conservative is not a reflection on your abilities as an investor. Every military general, every athlete, male or female, gets more conservative when they are ahead and the game is virtually won. In fact, not getting more conservative would be foolish.

You have a certain amount of money right now. What advice would you give your best friend in the same situation? Don't blow it, right? When Serena Williams is at game point, she remains keenly alert, aware and even aggressive, but she may not take the same chances she took in the opening set. When Joe Flacco or Payton Manning have the lead with three minutes to go in a playoff game, they don't pass on every down. They adapt, and move to the strategy with the highest percentage chance of winning. They run out the clock on the real enemy: failure. They take what the opposition is willing to give. They win because they adapt. So can you.

> **"The measure of intelligence is the ability to change."**
>
> — Albert Einstein

Look Ma, No Pension! A Symptom of the New Normal

People spend the first half of their lives accumulating money and paying into savings. They spend the second half of their lives trying to preserve their money and taking out of savings. In the past, 30 years on the job was rewarded with a pension. Today, the 401(k) and 403b has taken over. If you are going to have a pension, you will have to buy one on your own.

Research by the Center for A Secure Retirement found that two-thirds of middle-income Boomers believe their retirements will be different from that of previous generations. What will cause the difference? Pensions for one, debt for the other. Pensions and guaranteed income are what 60 percent of middle-income Boomers say they envy most about the retirement of previous generations.

In retirement, achieving a sustainable, reliable, guaranteed income is the most important goal of the investor.

Investing for Income: It's Different From Investing For

Accumulation

Here's the problem: Most traditional investments are based on the concept of capital appreciation. You buy assets, such as shares of stock, and hope they appreciate in value so you can sell them later for a profit. Cash-flow investing works differently. With cash flow, you buy an asset not for its future value but for its ability to generate income. This income gives you flexibility: You can spend it if you want to or you can reinvest it. Cash flow reinvested is compounding growth. In my financial planning system, we use reinvested dividends for growth in a separate bucket. We use annuities in the growth bucket. The annuity is a stabilizer for your entire investment plan. You can't build a house without a foundation.

The Need For A Guaranteed Lifetime Income Has Never Been Greater

Some retirees will go back to working a job during retirement and like the idea. Others may be forced to do so because finances are running thin, but it is unlikely they will find the kind of work and kind of money they are hoping for. If 25 and 35-year-olds are having trouble finding work, 65 and 70-year-olds won't fare much better.

Your money has to last and it has to work hard. But what income-generating product can be counted on to be there, come what may, good markets and bad?

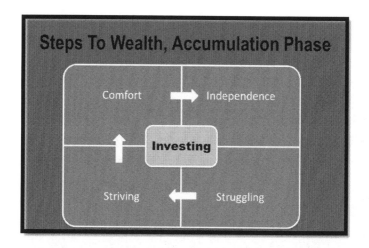

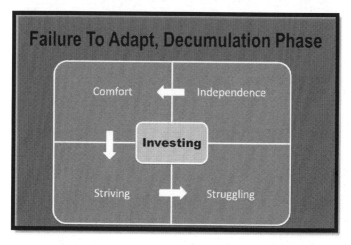

Frank Was In Danger Of Becoming A "Middle Class Millionaire"— And He Knew It.

Frank had an advantage: He was an engineer with a math background. Even though he was self-admittedly in denial for nearly eight years, after losing a half million dollars, he finally "got it." Money disappears fast when you are no longer making contributions but instead withdrawing. It is alarming. It is surprising. And when the money is gone, there is nothing you can do but adapt. At that point, you have a big decision to make:

1. Dial up the risk as some in the popular media suggest (it's always easier to risk others' money!).
2. Move to safer, income generating assets. Sometimes the only way to deal with a risk is to avoid it completely. It's not a sign of a bad investor, it's the sign of a good one, and it's called adapting. You're calling an audible at the line of scrimmage.

Unfortunately, many investors remain in denial and are shocked when they find that half a million or a million dollars does not provide automatic security. Income and preservation are not just worthy goals, they are the weaponry of financial survivors and thrivers. In the future, your income will be more important than your total assets.

In fact, the stronger your income, the more you can count on holding onto your assets.

The IQ Wealth Smarter Bucketing System™ can restore precision and predictability to your permanent retirement plan and can work in any economy—up, down, or sideways.

"It is not the strongest of the species that survives, nor the most intelligent, but the one most responsive to change."

-Charles Darwin

It's not what happens to you, but how you react to it that matters.

-Epictetus

Enter through the narrow gate. For wide is the gate and broad is the road that leads to destruction, and many enter through it. But small is the gate and narrow the road that leads to life, and only a few find it.

-Matthew 7:13-14

CHAPTER 2

WHEN YOU'RE READY FOR RETIREMENT, WILL RETIREMENT BE READY FOR YOU? HOW TO RETIRE AND STAY RETIRED

WHEN BABY BOOMERS WERE GROWING UP and growing their hair, people said "these kids don't know what they want." Today, Baby Boomers are becoming very clear about what they want in their financial plans: No BS, guaranteed sustainable income, simplified plans that are easy to understand, reduced fees, low risk, and upside growth potential. Did I mention *no BS?*

They want to retire and stay retired. This generation told their parents to quit worrying so much and enjoy life a little. Now, it's their turn-- they want to stop worrying and stop watching the market chew up their money. They're ready for a hybrid financial vehicle that can perform more than one task.

Like a hybrid car, hybrid "next generation" annuities combine income horsepower with durable, low-cost efficiency. Don't necessarily think "Prius" when you think "hybrid." There just so happen to be altima's, and honda's and Tesla's that have plenty of oomph that you can compare from. You just need to know where to look, and what to look for.

Retirees are looking at themselves in the mirror and realizing that two things are true: their time on this planet is limited, and their time could last another 20, 30, or 40 years.

For upper-middle-class couples in their 60s today, there's a 43%

chance that one or both will survive to at least age 95, according to the Society of Actuaries, which recently updated its mortality tables. By 2029, the odds of a 65-year-old reaching 95 climb to 50%.

But here's the problem: if you keep investing in unpredictable markets and low paying bonds and money markets, how do you know your money will last? How do you know you will always be able to live the same lifestyle?

Thinking people like to plan. They want to know their results in advance when it comes to their money. Life is more fun when it is spontaneous, but to be spontaneous you need money coming in every month. You can't have fun in life if you are worried about your investments.

Though we have all heard the phrase "cash is King", the phrase needs a little work when your retire. Cash FLOW is king when you are no longer getting a paycheck from work.

The simple definition of financial success in retirement is: "more money coming in than going out, from now on, no matter what."

People who have worked for what they have don't like risking it until they know their bills are all paid. Why not build a financial plan that will pay all your bills even if you and your spouse live well into your nineties.

Making annuities part of your overall plan can be stabilizing factor you are looking for. Its like buying an extra pension, yet you stay in control of your principal with the newer annuities.

Retired investors know they have many 10,000 options for their money at Fidelity or Vanguard, but most of them have too much risk. Only annuities can give you the income guarantees you are searching for, without principal market risk.

Now you know why annuities are rising in demand for the 50+ retirement minded person. The annuities of old are a thing of the past. Today's annuities are logical. They take an unknown and turn it into a known.

Stock brokers and "annuity haters" (who have their own agenda by the way) would prefer you not think logically.

They just want you to keep getting in line with the herd, and keep most of your money at risk. Can you really afford that in these turbulent times

CHAPTER 3

SOCIAL SECURITY: 5 MYTHS, 5 REALITIES, AND 5 LEGITIMATE REASONS FOR TAKING IT EARLY

When You Should Take Social Security: 5 Myths, 5 Realities

SOCIAL SECURITY, AS MUCH AS WE MIGHT GRIPE about the system as a whole, is still the financial foundation in retirement for well over 98% of all Americans. Most likely it is near the center of your retirement strategy. Steady, reliable income from as many sources as possible is what determines whether a plan will last or fall apart. Because Social Security is so important to our financial plans, it is not illogical to worry about the program going broke!

The concern, of course, is that our rising government debt, coupled with a trend toward social benefit expansion (if not downright socialism!), and the fact that fewer workers are supporting more and more benefit receivers, simply is no longer adding up. In fact, it is causing a drawdown of the Social Security trust fund, which supplies almost 25% of every social security check that goes out. The fund is scheduled to be completely depleted in 2034. So you are wise to make sure you have plan 'B' sources of income. The year 2034 is now no farther away than the year 2004. You remember back "that far", right?

We know that politicians will kick the can down the road until they are forced to do something about it, then blame the other side for why it got that bad. That's already baked into the cake, but you and I are problem solvers. We need to put a plan together now that will endure what may be coming our way. Social Security does have some serious stress points that need to be addressed. Those stress points could turn into serious cracks.

That said, there are several "Myths" about Social Security you want to be aware of. Here are five of those myths, with background and insight:

Myth No. 1:Social Security is running out of money and will go completely broke soon.

Ok, there is both good news and bad news here, but it is not as bad as it could be! True the trust fund will run out at some point, but money from workers will still be coming in. Here's a fact you need to know: The Social Security trust funds have been running a surplus in every year since 1982. Surpluses stopped in late 2018. The Social Security trust fund has a few trillion dollars in it, but the draw down need is great and getting greater. At a certain point, the Social Security system can rely on incoming interest payments from the treasury bonds they own to make up the deficit — for a while.

According to several government estimates, Social Security funds are likely to be depleted by 2034 — if no changes are made. If that happens, payment checks won't disappear, but they'll likely shrink by approximately 25%, leaving income recipients with about 75% of what they were expecting. That's better than zero– but the more affluent you are, the more you should be worried about the benefit being cut via "means testing." Means testing refers to the idea that the more wealthy Americans will see their benefits cut due to being "too successful." College campuses are pushing socialism and railing against "evil" capitalism. Many people fear that capitalism will give way to European socialism over time as the voting majority gets more liberal, and more in need of government support. That could be a real challenge.

Of course, there's a chance that the system will be shored up, one way or another. There are many possible fixes, though politicians don't agree on them, and by the looks of things might never agree! For example, fully 77% of the trust funds' shortfall could be eliminated by increasing the Social Security tax rate for employers and employees from its current 6.2% to 7.2% in 2022 and 8.2% in 2052. But--Which politician is ready to step up and raise taxes? Votes will be lost for that "hero."

Congress rarely agrees on anything unless there is a huge crash, like 2008, or a terror strike like 9-11. The odds are not good that a "Spartacus Moment" will overtake a highly influential senator who pushes to overhaul Social Security. Nobody on the Hill wants to risk their political career over that idea.

BUT the odds are good that taxes *could* be raised on Social Security benefits for more affluent Americans, and not just the super-rich. It would not be outlandish to think that anyone making $80,000 a year or more could pay progressively more in Social Security tax, and those making over $250,000 could really have to pay in more. Which brings us to "means testing." Means testing refers to the idea that the more you have, the less you need to receive the benefits you paid for. A "wealth tax" is also in the offing, meaning you could have Big Brother monitoring your assets constantly to determine how much tax you will pay on what you have already accumulated. On a likelihood scale, the idea of tapping into the so-called "rich" could become very popular once Democrats find their way back into power, which like it or hate it, is inevitable. If you lean Democrat, be careful what you wish for. If you lean Republican, hold onto your wallet, and build up your "AFORI"--Alternative Forms Of Retirement Income.

Myth No. 2: "The money you pay into the system is the money you receive from it later."

Some people assume that when money is removed from their paycheck, it goes into an account expressly for them — growing in value over time to provide them with income for retirement. Obviously, that's not true. Your money is pooled. The taxes from all the paychecks of people currently working are pooled and then paid out to retirees collecting their benefits.

So your contributions are supporting others, and when you retire your benefits will come from the earnings of those working. That has been a great system for a long time, but now there are cracks in the foundation. A) People are living longer and collecting benefits for more years. B) There are fewer workers supporting a growing number of retirees. Back in 1960, the contributing-workers-to-beneficiaries ratio was 5 to 1, with about 73 million workers supporting close to 14 million beneficiaries.

As of 2013, it was just 2.8 workers for every recipient (with 163 million workers supporting 57 million beneficiaries) — and it's expected to hit 2.1 by 2035, when the system will be out of reserves. These factors are stressing the system, making eventual changes to it probable—but once again it may be the usual fix: management by crisis. Politicians always have more courage during emergencies and chaos when no one can be blamed. Once again, hold onto your wallet and develop AFORI.

Which brings us to Myth No. 3: "Everyone contributes equally to Social Security."

We know that's not true because many people in the United States don't pay federal taxes because they make under $45,000 a year. They may be paying into FICA at the same tax rate for Social Security — but it's only up to a certain capped annual earnings amount. As of 2018, the new cap is $132,900. Thus, someone earning $132,900 in 2018 and someone earning $5 million will pay the same Social Security tax — a fact that many see as unfair, especially on the left side of the aisle. Which is why you must consider it a strong possibility if the Democrats control the executive office and both houses of Congress one day.

Myth No. 4: "The Social Security benefits you receive are based on your last 10 years of income."

Here's the deal: your benefits are based on the income you earned in your 35 highest-earning working years (adjusted for inflation). The rules do require you to accumulate 40 work credits in order to qualify for benefits, however, which is typically achieved in 10 years. If you've only worked 30 years, the formula will include five years' worth of zeroes, which will give you smaller benefit checks than if you'd worked for 35 years. If you work for more than 35 years, your lowest-earning years will be dropped, so working a little longer can be a way to boost your benefits—and perhaps the best way. There are very few fancy claiming strategies left. Building a bigger social security base for the higher earner makes sense because one day, the surviving spouse will have only the larger social security income to draw from.

Myth No. 5: "Social Security is designed to replace MOST of your pre-retirement income.... "

Nope, this one is not true at all. According to the Social Security Administration, retirement benefits for those with average earnings will likely replace about 40% of your pre-retirement earnings, give or take. Those who had above-average earnings in their working years can expect a lower replacement rate, and vice versa. The average monthly retirement benefit was recently $1,364 dollars per month, which amounts to $16,368 per year. If your earnings have been above average, though, you'll collect more than that — up to the maximum monthly Social Security benefit for those retiring at their full retirement age, which was recently $2,687 dollars, or about $32,000 for the whole year. So, if you are spending $5,000 to $10,000 a month, you are going to need to get more income from somewhere. The problem, bond funds are now risky, as is the stock market. Should you consider an annuity to supplement your Social Security? Many people are doing just that. Because pensions are fewer and farther between than ever, many engineers, teachers, business owners, and professionals are converting part of their 401(k) rollovers into qualified lifetime income annuities within their IRA rollovers.

The Bottom Line: "Should you start taking Social Security benefits early (at 62), or wait until the income hits the max?"

Hearing all that could go wrong in the next ten to fifteen years, many people are moved to take their benefits early. Starting the income early is not necessarily bad, although you will be told by 35 year old journalists on the internet that you should always wait until you hit your 70th birthday. I don't just believe that's false, I know it's false as a financial planner with more than 20 years of helping people retire.

Here are three good reasons for taking your Social Security early:

1. You find yourself drawing down on important retirement assets, leaving you exposed to financial shortfalls in your 80s or even 90s

2. You want to live more and do more fun things in your 60s while you are still healthier and more youthful.

3. Your genetics or current health point to a potentially shorter life span

4. You are emotionally convinced that Social Security will not be there for you one day

5. You have plenty of AFORI (Alternative Forms Of Retirement Income)

Six of One, Half Dozen of The Other

Remember, the system is actuarial and purely math-based--like a pension plan. If everyone dies on the same day, and that day is the average date of death for all Americans, then it doesn't matter a bit when you start your Social Security. You will get the same amount of money starting at age 62, 66, or 70. The bottom line: know your alternatives, and "what ifs". It is smart to work with an advisor who specializes in planning retirements. You need to know where every dollar of income needed to fund your lifestyle and handle emergencies is going to come from. An analysis of your projected spending needs against an overlay of future inflation is an indispensable part of the planning process. You will never have clarity, let alone serenity, unless you know how and when your living needs and lifestyle dreams will be covered from now on. That means you can never have too much AFORI.

Just a note before ending this chapter: there is no correct time for everyone to take their Social Security benefit. It could be 62, 66, or 70. Meet with someone who can show you the options. Get your income foundation built and built right.

"When the moon hits your eye like a big pizza pie,

that's amore' "

-Dean Martin

"When the money hits your account for the rest of your life never missing a beat,

that's AFORI"

-Steve Jurich, AIF®

CHAPTER 4

HAS THE "DEATH CROSS" ARRIVED FOR FIXED INCOME INVESTORS?

WHAT HAPPENS IF STOCKS AND BONDS both go down at the same time? Has the "Death Cross" arrived for Fixed Income, Target Date, ETF, and Life Cycle Investors?

This is truly a historic time to be an investor. Stocks have hit all-time highs, and bonds have hit all-time lows. A "cross" in value occurred on the way up. Investors in both stocks and bonds over the past 30 years have been rewarded fairly well. Very few people actually buy and hold and never touch their portfolios, so it is probably a rare investor who has the same stocks and bonds today as he or she held 30 years ago. When these trends reverse—when stocks start heading down and interest rates start heading up, retired investors will face what some call a "Death Cross" in a retirement portfolio, if the investor is taking regular withdrawals.

There have only been two other times in market history that both stocks and bonds suffered bear markets at the same time: 1931 and 1969. The setup is even more apparent today than in either of those two years:

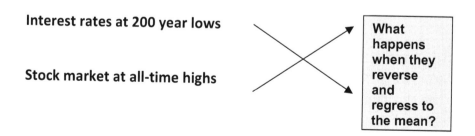

Interest rates at 200 year lows

Stock market at all-time highs

What happens when they reverse and regress to the mean?

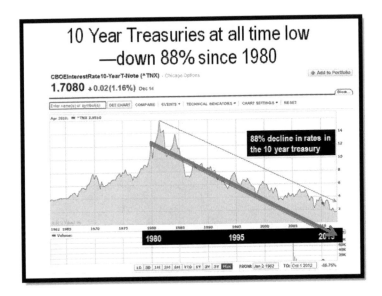

These figures were valid as of February 1, 2013. Contact an annuity professional for an update to current rates and terms. For additional advice, visit www.MyAnnuityGuy.com.

The Fixed Income Death Cross and Other Symptoms of the New Normal

(1)Stocks have become commodities—the average holding period for stocks is similar to commodity holding periods.

Dividends on stocks have been cut in half since 1990, and are virtually negated by fees.

(2) What dividends remain are not being reinvested by most investors.

(3) Investor mistakes: Investors continue to hold when they shouldn't, buy when they shouldn't, and sell when they shouldn't. Investors are investing in imperfect markets, using imperfect assets and tools, with imperfect knowledge of outcomes, finite resources and finite time, applied to an imperative need for permanent income

(4) Bonds have become commoditized through the use of ETFs and

Mutual Funds.

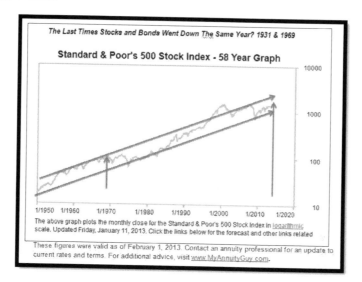

The Last Times Stocks and Bonds Went Down The Same Year? 1931 & 1969

Standard & Poor's 500 Stock Index - 58 Year Graph

The above graph plots the monthly close for the Standard & Poor's 500 Stock Index in logarithmic scale. Updated Friday, January 11, 2013. Click the links below for the forecast and other links related

These figures were valid as of February 1, 2013. Contact an annuity professional for an update to current rates and terms. For additional advice, visit www.MyAnnuityGuy.com.

(5) The "Death Cross" for fixed income investors has arrived: Bond interest rates reached their 200 year low in the fall of 2012, and stocks reached their 200 year high in February of 2013.

(6) Bonds and stocks are no longer automatic diversification vehicles. The setup for both to decline simultaneously is at its historic peak— both could fall precipitously, simultaneously. This makes diversification using stocks and bonds to offset each other potentially an exercise in futility. Both have migrated into being one "system" of pricing, and therefore subject to systematic risk. Systematic risk is un-diversifiable using assets in the system.

(7) Stocks could fall due to valuation risks, event risk, economic risk, and the acceleration of selling during a decline wrought by high frequency trading, which now dominates 70 percent of all trades on the New York Stock Exchange. A key issue is that the driving force of the 1990s bull market, Baby Boomers and the Silent Generation totaling 90 million adults, is moving to the de-cumulation phase and will be living off assets rather than contributing more to markets.

(8) Longer lifespans and medical advances combined with the lack of pensions and strains on social security means that near perfect investment results will need to be achieved by investors.

In 2013, the market wants to eat your money--bond fund mutual funds and ETFs want to swallow your cash.

Just as easily as the 9 percent to 15 percent gains from your bond funds thrilled you from 2009 to 2012, a corresponding capital loss is baked into the cake when interest rates go back to "normal." It can make your head hurt to think about it, but trust me, this is something you need to get. Bond funds and ETFs will swallow your cash one day if you let them.

When the economy recovers, bond-related losses will truly be a shock for many unsuspecting investors. Following suit, rising interest rates most likely will attract capital from the stock market into the safer havens of bank accounts with higher rates. Your stock mutual funds may start seeing dramatic outflows, leading to declining net asset values. Yes, both stock mutual funds and bond mutual funds can fall at the same time, and it can happen quite quickly. It may be a bit over-dramatic to call it the "Death Cross," but for now, that's my story and I'm sticking to it. I want you to have a healthy respect, if not fear, for this seemingly innocuous "pre-regression" to the mean.

This Ain't No Drill - A Former Navy Seal Reveals How To Avoid The Financial Death Cross: "C.H.E.A.T."

Clearly, investors find themselves in a dilemma today. Most are unaware of the risks, or are whistling past the graveyard. On the other hand, rising numbers of retirees are moving their 401(k), 403b, and IRA rollovers into Hybrid Index annuities, finally realizing that what the market can give, it can also take away. While the media might question the intelligence of this wave of annuity buyers— who are engineers, teachers, business owners, medical professionals, accountants and more-- I can tell you from personal experience that the most strident critics would have a hard time keeping up with the brainpower of many new annuity owners. Smart may indeed be the new rich.

I met a financial planner some years back, named Mike, who had been a Navy Seal. He told me that his philosophy in the world of money was similar to his experiences in military conflict. As he aptly pointed out, you can lose a game of Parcheesi or golf, and just tee it up again afterwards. In the battlefield, it doesn't work that way. If you lose to the guy in front of you, your teeing days are over. It's the same with your money. You have finite time and finite resources. When that money is gone and you need income again next month, you may have to take less than you wanted, and you may have to like it—for a long time. Not so with a hybrid index annuity strategy. Mike the military man had an acronym for winning battles you can't afford to lose. He called it the C.H.E.A.T. strategy:

Create

Highly

Effective

Alternative

Techniques

I submit to you that your retirement money is too important to leave to chance. You are a prudent person. You look to manage your money in the best way possible. You were probably raised during a time when common sense was praised as a personal trait. You shop at Costco, and Target, and Wal-Mart for some things, even if you like Nordstrom's and Neiman Marcus for others. You like saving a buck wherever and whenever you can. Then why wouldn't you save yourself from thousands in potential losses and fees, while locking in solid, sustainable income at lower cost?

You Can C.H.E.A.T. Death: Survive the Death Cross with

Diversification

Systematic Risk is not diversifiable unless you choose investments or assets from "outside the system." Stock funds and bond funds may be separate subsystems, but they fall under the category of being in the same mega system. If massive redemptions start occurring from either side of the aisle, stock funds or bond funds, you will quickly find that some of your prize possession funds and ETFs will need to be liquidated in order to meet redemption requests. Therefore, if all of your money is in mutual funds, whether stock funds, bond funds, balanced funds, target date funds, or life cycle funds, you are not fully and properly diversified in the truest sense. Your assets still may have too much "correlation" to one another.

To become truly diversified, you need to hold a solid block of assets, separate from mutual funds, that are non-correlated to the rest of your portfolio.

The assets you choose to diversify away from mutual funds should be functional and efficient, in other words have utility. They should perform a function that the rest of your portfolio can't or won't. The properly chosen Hybrid annuity builds L.U.C.K into your portfolio:

Liquidity

Utility

Control

Knowledge

You couldn't pick a better time than right now to make the move to safety and security. Your bond fund values may never be higher - and your stock market positions may be higher one day, but also could be setting up for a fall. No one knows, but this is not the time in your life for "woulda, coulda, or shoulda."

As John Bogle said about stocks, there comes a day when the wave

hits the shore. Don't be there waiting for it. Create highly effective alternative techniques instead.

Many investors make the mistake of equating liquidity with safety. Your portfolio should be arranged to include six to 18 months of living expenses in the form of liquid capital, depending on your circumstances.

This will allow you to use more effective instruments that may be only partially liquid, but are far more effective than cash accounts at achieving the portfolio's objectives of income and growth. While bond funds and ETFs seem to have a comfortable amount of liquidity, in truth there are risk trade-offs that can damage a long term plan. Let's explore some of the important risks found in traditional investments.

Understanding The Risks of Traditional Investments

Type of Risk	What Is It?	What Common Investments Carry It?
Market Risk	The risk that random market behavior will reduce the value of an asset without warning.	Stocks, stock mutual funds and ETFs, publicly traded REITS, variable annuity sub accounts.
Short Maturity Risk	The risk that an investment will mature at a time of lower interest rates and that the funds must be reinvested at lower yields.	Bank CDs, short term bonds, Ginny Mae's, fixed annuities.
Marketability Risk	The risk that an asset cannot be sold quickly at current market prices without depressing the market and accepting a lesser price.	Non Traded REITs, real estate rentals, Oil and Gas limited partnerships, Private Equity deals, TICs.
Additional Commitment Risk	The risk that an investor will be forced to commit additional funds to an investment, should certain conditions occur that are beyond the investor's control. If the additional investment is not made, the investment may be subject to losses.	Real estate rentals, TICs, some limited partnerships, and margin calls on market based assets. Any time an additional commitment of funds is required to restore value in any investment.
Call Risk	The risk that the issuers of callable bonds and preferred stock will redeem them when comparable market rates fall significantly below the rates paid by the bonds or preferreds.	Callable Municipal bonds, corporate bonds, bond funds and ETFs, preferred stock that is callable.
Redemption and Reinvestment Risk	The risk that you won't be able to get your money out of a mutual fund or REIT when you want, and in the amount you want.	Mutual funds, non-traded REITS, limited partnerships.
Sequence of Returns Risk	The risk that a bad order of returns combined with income withdrawals can deplete a portfolio at an accelerated pace. This is increases longevity risk.	Stocks, REITS, Stock and bond mutual funds and ETFs, variable annuity sub accounts.

CHAPTER 5

ARE YOU ALL THUMBS?

HOW OUTMODED RULES OF THUMB MAY LEAD TO FINANCIAL RUIN—ESPECIALLY WITH BOND FUNDS

WE ALL DO IT. I'VE DONE IT. You and I will both do it again. What is it? Making dumb mistakes based on old rules of thumb. There are many comfy, familiar rules of the road that have served us well in the past, in life and investing. The key to lasting investment success is not following old rules of thumb – but making sure your investments are in-line with your principles.

The trouble with rules of thumb is not that they are all wrong, but that it is so easy to misapply them, or to apply them at the wrong times. Rules of thumb are Band-Aids when major surgery is required. When it comes to retirement investing, dumb mistakes cost money. The biggest mistake that a retired investor can make right now is believing they are safely diversified in a pile of bond mutual funds or bond ETFs. Even FINRA has issued on alert on bond risk. The evidence is clear: If you are using bond mutual funds or bond ETFs as the preservation strategy for your retirement, you are very likely making a D.U.M.B. mistake.

Diversifying

Under

Misguided

Beliefs

It's too late in the game for D.U.M.B. mistakes

I like the Boy Scout motto, "Be Prepared," for many reasons. I was a boy scout and proud of it. Life has proven to me that *"pre*-paring" is so much easier than *"re*-pairing." Looking under the hood of your portfolio right now, are there any dumb mistakes waiting to happen? Are you using rules of thumb rather than sound principles?

Some Rules of Thumb are useful and can help investors stay on track. Others are simply misguided beliefs and can cost you real money at the wrong time of your life.

Getting away from the nonsense, there are two kinds of people:

1. Those who spend first and save the difference, and
2. Those who save first and spend what's left.

Guess which group retires better, regardless of what other Rules of Thumb they follow?

If you must rely on Rules of Thumb, here's a tip:

Be cautious when you hear the words "always" and "never."

That said, here are some reasonable Rules of Thumb:

- Pay yourself first. Set aside your savings every month before you use the money for other things, including bills.

- Always take the employer match on the 401(k).

- Never touch your retirement savings — except for retirement.

- Never co-sign on a loan.

- In general, save an emergency fund first; pay off high-interest debt second; and begin investing (at the same time you pay down remaining debt) last.

- Save 10 percent of your income.

- An emergency fund should equal 3 months of your expenses (I like at least 12).

- 100 – Your Age = The amount you should have invested in stocks.

- Invest no more than 10 percent of your total savings in your employer's stock.

- In retirement, you'll need to replace 80 percent of your pre-retirement income.

- Life insurance should equal 5 times your income (or 8 or 12 times).

Rules of Thumb (R.O.T.) That Can Get You Into Trouble

- Especially when you combine *two* Rules of Thumb into *one*, and decide it's a "strategy":

- **"As long as you withdraw only 4 percent annually, you'll always be fine."** (Wrong! This one is the biggest whopper on the page.)

- **"Stocks Always Make 10 percent."** (Reality check: Between 1981 and 1998, when the stock market was averaging annual returns of almost 13 percent, this figure seemed conservative. Since then, the stock market has seen the bursting of the dot-com bubble, followed by a second crash in 2008, and the drop we're enduring even now. According to some experts, the stock market may return as little as 4.5 percent annually going forward.)

- **"If you hold *stocks* for 25 years, you can't make less than 7.9 percent."** (Define "stocks" – Almost no one buys and holds the S&P 500 for 25 years. Once active management or tinkering is applied to the portfolio, you can throw the stats on "stocks" out the window.)

- **"If you hold "stocks for 15 years, you can't lose"** (Define "stocks"!)

- **"Prior to retirement, save eight times your annual salary."** (You'd better invest it well—you or your spouse may spend 35 to 40 years in retirement. I've also heard "save 25 times salary." Sure, nothing to it, lol. Do they mean 25 times in today's dollars or future dollars?)
- **"Bonds are safe."** (Bonds held in bond funds or ETFs are not principal protected. Most of the R.O.T. on bonds refers to ACTUAL bonds, and to an era when they paid 5% to 7%)
- **"You can't lose money in bonds."** (When interest rates rise on the street, the value of your bond funds can head straight down.)
- **"Prior to retirement, save 25 times your annual salary"** (Guess what? You can still screw it up with a poor sequence of returns and steady withdrawals.)
- **"Prior to retirement, save 12 times your annual salary."** (I hope you're getting the point here. Each of these rules of thumb is from high sources and can readily be found on the internet. Knowing you need either 8, 12, or 25 times earnings should clear things up! REALITY CHECK: Net worth is just a snapshot in time. Coordinating spending and investment performance is the key.)
- **"The Market Always Comes Back"** (Unless you're withdrawing income.)
- **"Don't Worry, You're In It For The Long Run"** (That's the problem.)

CRAZY Rules of Thumb - Hey, they probably work as well as some of the rules above:

- If the palm of your right hand itches, you'll soon be coming into money. If your left palm itches you'll soon be paying out money. (Full disclosure: My mom believed this one and it is a hard one for me to shake)

- If three people are photographed together, the one in the middle will die first. (Fortunately, this is not how life insurance policies are determined)

- A cow lifting its tail is a sure sign that rain is coming. (Stand clear!)

- If you're lucky enough to see the first flower of springtime on a Friday, it's a sign of impending wealth. (hmmm, get out the tent, we're going camping)

- An itchy nose is a sign someone is coming to see you. If it's the right side, the visitor will be female; the left side, male.(Which one for the IRS?)

With the IQ Wealth Smarter Bucketing System™, you won't need Rules of Thumb. Your income and preservation plan will be

Specific

Measured

Attainable

Reliable

Timely

CHAPTER 6

BOND BASICS – HOW MONEY IS MADE AND LOST IN BOND FUNDS, BOND ETFS, AND TARGET DATE MUTUAL FUNDS

Reclaim Ownership of Your Retirement

A BOND IS A LOAN, AN IOU. When a company or governmental agency needs to raise capital, it can borrow money from investors by issuing bonds that can be bought as securities. A bond has a coupon rate—the rate of interest—and a maturity date when you can get back all your principal. Most bonds pay interest every six months until maturity. High quality bonds are considered investment grade, while "high yield" bonds are considered non-investment grade and nicknamed "junk" bonds. High quality, investment grade bonds are Will Rogers' idea of a good investment: a return on your money and a return *of* your money. Everyone wants the perfect investment. It can't be found now, but may have actually existed for a few years: The 30 year U.S. Treasury paid 13 percent to 15 percent in 1980. The risk-adjusted return was off the charts.

If you're going to reclaim ownership of your retirement, you're going to need to own assets that will not turn around and bite you when the "new normal" starts moving back to the "old" normal. Cycles are part of life and economics. The tide always turns. For you, I don't want it to be when you are lying on a hammock in your back yard or taking that summer cruise to Alaska you've been planning.

Read The Ingredients, Not Just The Label

Bonds are not risk free, even when you are holding the actual bonds in your portfolio. But when you only hold title to bond mutual funds and ETFs, the bonds aren't yours. You own shares. Your shares are a commoditized form of bonds, but not bonds. Your shares are interest sensitive on a day-to-day basis. The average interest rate on 10 year treasuries for the past century is around 5.8 percent. When interest rates hang around those levels, there's no problem. In fact, when bond rates are at 6 percent or so, bond funds and bonds are nearly identical. That's why all this business about interest rate risk is new to most investors. It's been a non-issue for a long time.

Even more fun, when interest rates are in a long down trend and falling, your bond funds and ETFs will be your prize possessions. They will rise to new heights in trading value! Total returns of between 9 percent and 15 percent may be the norm. The interest earned will be slim, but the capital gains will be high. You may glow with enthusiasm about the strategist who picked these out for you.

Well, two out of three ain't bad, because when interest rates revert to normal, after a long trend down (let's say 30 years or so), bonds and bond funds go their separate ways. They no longer look like each other, or act like each other. If you are still holding onto the bond funds when this shift occurs, the 9 percent to 15 percent capital gains can turn into 9 percent and 25 percent capital losses. The longer the duration of the bonds, the worse the losses, in fact. You can switch to shorter term funds in the meantime, but your returns will become paltry or your risk increased through the use of more junk bonds. Complex? Yes.

Bonds are well known for Interest Rate Risk. Bond mutual funds and bond ETFs add the element of Systematic Risk. Essentially, when interest rates rise, bond values fall. If you own the bond, you can choose to hold until maturity. But not if you own bond ETFs, Target Dates, or Bond Funds. Your account's value falls that day. Bonds and bond funds no longer play by the same rules. The plan "B" that comes with ownership of the maturity, is lost when you own the fund. The real issue: in a major market meltdown, when you want to chill and just be safe, your bond funds or bond ETFs will likely be needed for redemptions.

This is why I urge my clients not to be "D.U.M.B." – please avoid **D**iversifying **U**nder **M**isguided **B**eliefs. Investing in bond funds and ETFs will simply not diversify your portfolio in the same way that a good old fashioned bond will.

Your Age In Bonds?

A famous Rule of Thumb is your "age in bonds" but notice the rule doesn't say, "your age in *temporary capital gain instruments* that rise in value when interest rates fall, and *fall in value when interest rates rise*." With bond funds and ETFs, you own shares of a complex instrument that is valued daily according to market forces and the direction of interest rates. The ETF or fund may even contain complex derivatives to hedge risk. The derivatives may have a hedging *effect*, but it's not an exact science. Very, very, very smart people invent and create derivatives. If you recall, derivatives were responsible for the 2008 melt down. Hedging a risk is better than ignoring it, but hedging is still a bet, plain and simple. The bet itself costs money, and the bet can be wrong. If you were thinking you owned a solid, stable, simple investment with a fund or ETF, think again. Therefore, putting your age into something more solid, like income annuities, is an idea that has gained traction.

Holding a bond to maturity is the bond owner's Plan B. As we've seen, the person or entity that owns title to the actual bonds is who owns the maturity date. **If that's not you, you don't own the right to hold the bond to maturity, i.e, you have no Plan B.**

The Age In Bonds rule is based on real live bonds, not funds. You can't choose to hold bonds you don't own.

Will the Traditional "60/40" Portfolio Save Your Retirement? The Evidence Is In. Think again.

Wall Street has long promoted keeping 60 percent of your money in stocks and 40 percent in bonds as the ultimate retirement strategy, claiming an average of 8 percent returns over time. Is that figure reliable, or is it a misguided belief?

Brett Arends of the *Wall Street Journal* became skeptical of the 60/40 portfolio strategy in 2011 and reported on data compiled by the Federal Reserve and analyzed by New York University's Stern School of Business. He created a hypothetical 60/40 portfolio and tracked it over the past 85 years, rebalancing it annually. In his words, the "average return of 8 percent" is full of holes. Most of the gains came in two booms: during the 1950s, and in the past 30 years—both downward trends in interest rates. For many other periods, the returns were meager, or nonexistent.

As Mr. Arends reports: "From January 1, 1937, through January 1, 1950, a period of 13 years, this surefire 60/40 portfolio, rebalanced annually, earned you absolutely nothing after inflation. Zip. The story was the same from 1965 to 1982 -- a slump that lasted nearly two decades. In the real world, investors did even worse than zero. They paid trading costs, fund-management fees and taxes."

Be wary of the idea of setting and forgetting a 60/40 bond portfolio. Once again, if both stock and bond markets simply move toward probability and head back toward normal levels, a 60/40 portfolio will be out in the open, in the line of fire.

Put A Concrete Floor Under Your 401k, 403b, or IRA Rollover.

Bond funds and ETFs offer temporary capital gains that can turn into permanent financial losses if interest first rise. Hybrid annuities are a new breed of cat can offer stable gains in value, but they prevent capital losses by taking them out of the picture. Hybrid annuities are not market instruments. They don't have anything to do with Wall Street except to benefit from well-known market indexes in the form of higher interest rates from time to time. They do not participate in any market losses and do not participate in losses due to interest rates rising. In fact, rising rates can help annuity owners in some ways.

Comparing modern day annuities to bond ETFs and funds goes something like this: Rather than basing your retirement on volatile assets that can result in permanent capital losses from a current regression to the mean, hybrid annuities may prevent capital losses and provide permanent stable income. **Since income is the focus in retirement, annuity owners are finding that sense of control they were missing.**

Target Date Funds: Loaded With Bond Risks and Hard Choices

Bond mutual funds are used heavily in a popular investment strategy known as Target Date Funds, also called Life Cycle Funds. In searching for a set-and-forget investment strategy, investors may land on target date mutual funds. Far from being a safe haven, target date funds are criticized for not protecting investors nearing retirement from major losses in 2008. They are often touted as the only retirement investment you'll ever need, however, experts increasingly are warning against the risks and the remarkable differences in the strategies among mutual fund purveyors.

Target funds are structured to protect investors by reducing exposure to stocks and increasing bond holdings as people get closer to retirement, which is called their "target" year. As we have just reviewed, however, increasing bond holdings at this historic stress point for bonds may be problematic. A target date fund can be described as a "fund of funds," which means you own many funds, not just one, and can have several layers unpredictability.

In "Target Funds Keep Falling Short" (01/22/2013) Jonnelle Marte reported in the *Wall Street Journal's Market Watch* that the average target date fund has only averaged 2 percent over the past five years.

> "...while the performance for these funds has been generally positive since the financial crisis, the average 2015 fund was up just 2 percent a year over the past five. Given that most financial-planning models assume annual returns of 6 percent

at a minimum, that shortfall can pose a significant problem for savers who rely on the funds."

For 2012, the average fund with a 2015 target date increased 10.6 percent, according to Morningstar Inc., a fund-research firm. That trails the Standard & Poor's 500-stock index, which rose 16 percent, but is well above the Barclays Capital Aggregate Bond Index's gain of 4 percent.

Diversification spreads risk, but it also reduces overall returns. The problem with Target Date funds is not apparent in strong markets like 2012. The weakness is exposed in flat markets and when retirees start withdrawing money to live on. Target date funds got crushed in 2008, and may get crushed in another major setback, specifically if a version of the "Death Cross" scenario occurs.

Part of the problem for older investors, say industry experts, is that the funds aren't designed to make up lost ground—especially as they near the target. "They're supposed to be conservative, so they aren't going to bounce back enough," says Ron Surz, president of Target Date Solutions.

Bringing A Knife To A Gunfight—Mutual Fund Portfolios May Be No Match For Sequence of Returns Risk and Reverse Dollar Cost Averaging

Five years ago, the term "sequence of return risk" was not even appearing in glossaries on investments. No one was really talking about it. Things have changed.

Investopedia Defines Sequence of Returns Risk:

> ## Sequence of Returns Risk, Today's #1 risk in retirement

"It is not just long-term average returns that impact your financial wealth, but the timing of those returns. When retirees begin withdrawing money from their investments, the returns during the first few years can have a major impact on their wealth.

Two retirees with identical wealth can have entirely different financial outcomes, depending on when they start retirement. A retiree starting out at the bottom of a bear market will have better investing success in retirement than another starting out at a market peak, even if the long-term averages are the same."

Although one popular Rule of Thumb is that 4 percent is a "safe" withdrawal rate, recent findings have proven that false. In an article titled "A Safer Safe Withdrawal Rate Using Various Return Distributions," published on the *Journal For Financial Planning* website (referenced from January 2013), Dr. Joseph M. Goebel and Dr. Manoj Athavale reported their findings that 4 percent may no longer be a safe withdrawal rate.

Overview of the Research Conducted By PhD's Athavale and Goebel:

- "A common conundrum faced by most people approaching retirement is the amount of money they can safely withdraw from their retirement portfolio without the risk of depleting the portfolio over their retirement horizon. The advice that most retirees will hear is the 4 percent rule—a retiree who faces normal retirement conditions can make an annual inflation-adjusted withdrawal equal to 4 percent of the original portfolio without risk of depleting the portfolio.
- This rule of thumb has helped bring a disciplined approach to retirement withdrawal strategy. However, tests of the 4 percent rule using simulation methodology have assumed that expected returns are drawn from a lognormal distribution—an assumption that lacks empirical support."
- Our analysis indicates that a 4 percent withdrawal rate will result in portfolio failure with greater probability (18 percent) than previously believed, and the truly "safe" withdrawal

rate—2.52 percent—is significantly smaller than previously believed.

Putnam Institute Warns of Sequence of Returns Risk In Target Date Funds

The most important shortcoming of target date funds is the lack of respect for Sequence of Returns Risk. Target date funds are already under attack for letting down shareholders during the 2008 market meltdown, but the first paper out from the Putnam Institute raises the question of whether even the most conservative target date funds are taking too much risk. W. Van Harlow, director of research at the Putnam Institute, claims that most Target Date funds should allocate as little as 10 to 12 percent of assets to equities.

The Putnam Institute is a research and educational organization funded by Putnam Investments. It aims to critically examine key investment theories, strategies and assumptions and suggest changes that can achieve better outcomes for companies, institutions, plans sponsors, investment advisors and individual investors. **Van Harlow says that, until recently, even he did not appreciate the role that sequence of returns plays in determining how long a person's nest egg will last in retirement.**

In a well circulated press release, the institute published these findings in a paper titled "Optimal Asset Allocation in Retirement: A Downside Risk Perspective." The study arrives at a series of conclusions that challenge conventional industry wisdom and practice, including:

- Most lifecycle fund offerings in today's market are too aggressive in their equity exposures: The appropriate range of equity allocation in retirement is between 5 percent and 25 percent (if an investor's primary goal is to not outlive his or her assets);

- Once an investor begins net withdrawals, the greatest risk to his or her portfolio becomes a potentially unfavorable "sequence of returns" — not inflation, or longevity;

- The onset of net withdrawals should be seen as any investor's "true" target date — and it should also mark the "terminal allocation" — the end of any roll-down or glide path; and,

- It makes no sense to continue rolling down equity exposure past anyone's true target date — and funds that do so are overly risky and misleading.

The most important aspect of mutual fund and ETF investing is whether you are *accumulating money for the future*, or *withdrawing money to live on*. Once you are withdrawing, the risk is on. **And the key risk for you, the retiree, according to the Putnam Institute, is the Sequence of Returns Risk.**

Let's look at how the sequence of returns can affect a $300,000 portfolio, using various withdrawal rates and the recorded returns of the S&P 500. Hypothetical for illustrative purposes only:

Scenario 1: 66 Year Old Retiree takes steady withdrawals at the "safe" withdrawal rate of 4%, with an early loss in the portfolio, similar to 2008.

On a hypothetical $500,000 portfolio. Retiree begins retirement with $500,000 balance and $20,000 level withdrawals. The following chart is indicative of "breaking even" the first year of retirement, then getting a poor sequence of returns—1998 to 2008—*in reverse.*

Year	Account Value	Market Result	GAIN/LOSS IN $	ACCOUNT VALUE	Management Fees @ 1.5%	Annual fees in dollars	Income Withdrawn 4%	TOTAL INCOME RECEIVED	End of Year ACCOUNT VALUE
1	$500,000	0%	0%	$500,000	$492,500	$7,500	$20,000	$20,000	$472,500
2	$472,500	-37%	-$174,825	$297,675	$293,210	$4,465	$20,000	$40,000	$273,210
3	$273,210	5%	$13,660	$286,870	$282,567	$4,303	$20,000	$60,000	$262,567
4	$262,567	16%	$42,011	$304,578	$300,009	$4,569	$20,000	$80,000	$280,009
5	$280,009	5%	$14,000	$294,010	$289,600	$4,410	$20,000	$100,000	$269,600
6	$269,600	11%	$29,656	$299,256	$294,767	$4,489	$20,000	$120,000	$274,767
7	$274,767	21%	$57,701	$332,468	$327,481	$4,987	$20,000	$140,000	$307,481
8	$307,481	-25%	-$76,870	$230,611	$227,152	$3,459	$20,000	$160,000	$207,152
9	$207,152	-11%	-$22,787	$184,365	$181,599	$2,765	$20,000	$180,000	$161,599
10	$161,599	-10%	-$16,160	$145,439	$143,258	$2,182	$20,000	$200,000	$123,258

Past performance is not a reliable indicator of future results. Year one is considering a zero return in the first year of retirement. Years 2-10 are the approximate returns—in reverse sequence— from 1998-2008. I.e., year two approximates 2008, year three 2007, year four 2006, year 5 2005, year 6 2004, year 7, 2003, year 8 2000, year 9 2001, year 10 2002.
Source: Yahoo, Standard & Poors

Scenario 2:   66 Year Old Retiree stops 4% withdrawals after 5 years, cutting withdrawals in half.

Retiree begins retirement with $500,000 balance, with an income need of $20,000 annually. This equals a 4% withdrawal rate.   After witnessing a depletion of investment balance to $269,600 in a mere five years, lowers withdrawals and shrinks lifestyle spending. At the end of ten years, retiree is ten years older. Portfolio has fallen from $500,000 to $162,478, with perhaps another 20 years of retirement to go.

Year	Account Value	Market Result	GAIN/LOSS IN $	ACCOUNT VALUE	Management Fees @ 1.5%	Annual fees in dollars	Income Withdrawn 4%	TOTAL INCOME RECEIVED	End of Year ACCOUNT VALUE
1	$500,000	0%	0%	$500,000	$492,500	$7,500	$20,000	$20,000	$472,500
2	$472,500	-37%	-$174,825	$297,675	$293,210	$4,465	$20,000	$40,000	$273,210
3	$273,210	5%	$13,660	$286,870	$282,567	$4,303	$20,000	$60,000	$262,567
4	$262,567	16%	$42,011	$304,578	$300,009	$4,569	$20,000	$80,000	$280,009
5	$280,009	5%	$14,000	$294,010	$289,600	$4,410	$20,000	$100,000	$269,600
6	$269,600	11%	$29,656	$299,256	$294,767	$4,489	$10,000	$110,000	$284,767
7	$284,767	21%	$59,801	$344,568	$339,399	$5,169	$10,000	$120,000	$329,399
8	$329,399	-25%	-$82,350	$247,050	$243,344	$3,706	$10,000	$130,000	$233,344
9	$233,344	-11%	-$25,668	$207,676	$204,561	$3,115	$10,000	$140,000	$194,561
10	$194,561	-10%	-$19,456	$175,105	$172,478	$2,627	$10,000	$150,000	$162,478

All figures approximate, returns are hypothetical based on reversing the sequence of returns between 1998-2008 after a zero return in the first year of retirement. I.E. years 2-12 approximate the returns from 2008-1998. Assumes 1.5% management fees. Past performance of any asset or index should never be relied upon to predict future results.

Even though this couple "tightened their belts", stopped traveling and "made ends meet", they still depleted their savings in a hurry. Poor planning is the problem here.

The Moral Of The Story Is That If You Are Retiring After A Long Run Up In Stocks, Be Careful and Be Realistic. Past Performance Definitely Does NOT Predict Future Returns.

In fact, reversion to the mean could serve to lower your returns as water seeks its own level in the markets.

Once you move from the accumulation and contribution phase to the preservation and withdrawal phase, a fluctuating portfolio has the opposite effect. During your working years, you are "buying on the dips" with each 401k contribution. When the market was down, and you kept contributing, you were buying more units of value with each contribution. After you stop working, you are no longer contributing. Rather than buying on the dips you are selling on the dips. If you get a bad sequence of returns while drawing a "safe" 4% annually, the results can be disastrous. If you ignore it, Sequence of Returns Risk can destroy an exposed portfolio.

The above charts not only "could happen", they did happen. It could be said that the crashes of 2000-2002 and 2008 were the natural and normal reaction to a record-breaking run up in stocks from 1983 to 1999. It has been shown that workers are more likely to "pull the plug" and retire when the markets hit a peak. It "feels good" because your balances are higher. Unfortunately, if you don't switch your investments to income and preservation from capital appreciation, you are asking for trouble. Getting your income from non-income producing assets means you have to sell assets to create your income. Not only is that complicated and hard to do, you may never feel confident to spend unless the markets are soaring. Why not hit the "easy button" instead?

The S.M.A.R.T. portfolio pays you the same great income whether the markets are going up, down, or sideways. Yes—it is possible to get your income from assets that are built to pay you from five to nine percent annually for life, depending on your age and deferral period. By separating your retirement nest egg into 4 buckets: 1) cash equivalents, 2) guaranteed income, 3) prudent long term growth, and 4) insurance needs (like LTC and life insurance), you get your dollars working harder and keeping your portfolio working more efficiently. You can still grow your money in the growth bucket, but you will be getting your income from assets built to pay you and never quit. Today with bonds paying so little, the stock market so uncertain, and pensions getting fewer and farther between, more and more smart professionals are taking matters into their own hands and using annuities as all or part of their IRA rollover from a 401k, 403b or 457 plan.

Annuities are part investment, part insurance. That's a good thing. They are designed as a tool for retirement and best suited for people age 45 to 85. Not all annuities are alike, so make sure you are comparing "apples to apples" and getting impartial information.

Key point: Beware of the heavy fees of *variable* annuities and beware of what are referred to as "Fixed Income" annuities sold at Fidelity and Vanguard. If you want to keep your fees low, your income high, your principal secure, and still have the potential to grow your money, you will find what you are looking for with carefully selected "Next Generation" fixed index annuities.

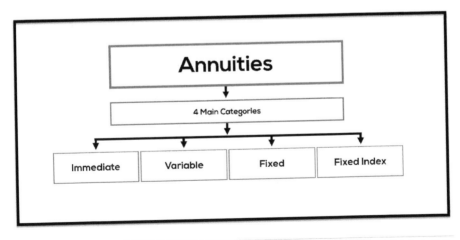

Note: The above spreadsheets are approximate and based roughly on published index returns for the years indicated. The intent is not to restate history with exactitude, but rather to illustrate concepts. All figures are approximate and for general conceptual information only. Past performance should never be relied upon to predict future results.

CHAPTER 7

PAST PERFORMANCE IS NO GUARANTEE OF FUTURE SUCCESS—

"HEY, THEY WEREN'T KIDDING!"

THE GREATEST DANGER FOR SOMEONE planning retirement is relying on past performance as a guide to future returns. If you are retiring after a big run up in the market (like the years ending in 1999 or 2019), the risk is that reversion to the mean will occur over the next ten years. Consider the market's return from 2000-2009, a ten year period with a negative result. Imagine what happens if you keep your faith in the market repeating itself upon retirement. Not good. With every prospectus and brochure on investments, these words will always appear: "Past performance is no guarantee of future results." They aren't kidding.

In 2000, the 11 percent loss was considered a "hiccup." After the 12 year run investors had been through, they felt experienced and hardened by the dusty trail. After all, there were entire weeks, and even months, that went by when stocks fell, yet they had persevered through those "tough times!" Advisors and investors kept repeating the phrase "The market always comes back". That strategy hadn't failed going back to 1983; who would believe it could fail now? Besides, at this point, most investors felt they were playing with the house's money, and if things got really bad, they could hop on the computer and get out of the markets. They would still be ahead and could jump back in when the market began to recover.

Because of the success of the strategy known as "buy-and-hold" it was common for investors to hold a combination of S&P 500, Nasdaq, and bond oriented mutual funds in 2000. Therefore, many portfolios may have approximated the average of the S&P in their portfolios. Although many possibilities exist, we'll consider the performance of the S&P 500 as an acceptable benchmark for purposes of illustration throughout this book. It may not be perfect but it can help us to understand the mathematical relationships involved in withdrawing money from market-reliant investments. Let's look at a chart that displays the retirement portfolio of the 67 year old engineer retiring January 1, 2000 believing they would continue to average 10% to 18% returns. They needed $40,000 annually from their investments to travel and pay their bills. Making money in the past like that, they figured they were being conservative withdrawing "only" 7.2%. The results weren't pretty: their account fell from $614,962 to $253, 931 in a matter of four short years.

Year	Account Value	Market Result	GAIN/LOSS in dollars	ACCOUNT VALUE	Management Fees @ 1.5%	Annual fees in dollars	Income Withdrawn 4%	TOTAL IN-COME RE-CEIVED	End of Year ACCOUNT VALUE
1999	$549,534	21%	$115,402	$664,936	$654,962	$9,974	$40,000	$280,000	$614,962
2000	$614,962	-18%	-$61,496	$553,466	$545,164	$8,302	$40,000	$320,000	$505,164
2001	$505,164	-12%	-$60,620	$444,544	$437,876	$6,668	$40,000	$360,000	$397,876
2002	$397,876	-25%	-$99,469	$298,407	$293,931	$4,476	$40,000	$400,000	$253,931

Past performance is not a reliable indicator of future results. These are the approximate returns Dec 31 1999-2002. Source: Yahoo, Standard & Poors

For additional input, visit **www.IQWealthManagement.com**

You might be asking why this couple kept withdrawing $40,000? 1) they needed that much to support the dreams they had settled planned on and 2) they believed "the market always comes back."

It Sounds Crazy, But Here's Why investors hang on to losing investments—even when account values are falling

Another question that is valid: why did the investor stayed with the same stock portfolio, even though it was losing money? Here's the problem: he was following the common conventional wisdom of "not panicking," and "staying the course." The advisor said not to worry. Unfortunately, that strategy doesn't work in a *decumulation* portfolio.

Because of his success during the previous 12 years, the 10 percent loss at the end of the first year was not a worry. After all, "The market always comes back", right? There was no reason to panic in his mind. Besides, he was "only" taking 7.2 percent, and after averaging well over 12 % for years. What could go wrong? Well, as you can see—plenty can go wrong when you put your faith in past performance. The world and the market are totally random. You never know. This couple's account went from $649k to $254k--with possibly another 20 to 30 years to go in retirement.

Your first reaction might be that he should have sold out after the first loss in 2000 - you and I agree. In fact, I had a very big year in 2000 as many people decided to take their money and run, moving their account balance into a high quality, carefully selected index annuity. They locked in all of their previous gains, and avoided the decline. Back then, income riders didn't exist. Today, we would be recommending a Next Generation Fixed Index annuity with a strong income rider, to achieve the 7.2% income for life, with no risk of market loss or income diminishment. Sadly, I spoke with people who were interested in the annuity concept, but were talked out of it by their brokers.

Unfortunately the example here is representative of many individuals who became anchored in their beliefs about the stock market from past performance. The study of behavioral finance would call this a case of becoming overconfident, and suffering from the "hot hand" fallacy. Those two factors gave him an "illusory sense of control"—all common frailties that come with being human.

Would the annuity decision have been sound and sensible? The short general answer is yes, but this investor should have had an outcome based income strategy before embarking on those generous withdrawals. By the way, let's not forget that 2008 was around the corner, a few miles ahead. Keeping a floor under his money would have prevented all losses during both the 2000 crash and the 2008 crash. He would have continued to benefit from upward market movements according to a formula and locked in gains as he went along. According to studies by the Wharton School of Business, index annuities in that time period averaged a respectable 6.32 percent return.

Rule of Thumb: "Diversify, Diversify, Diversify" Lesson: Diversification Spreads Risk But Does Not Eliminate It

Smart portfolios are diversified portfolios. No competent advisor would ever recommend you put all your eggs in one basket and invest your entire principal in one place. It's such an obvious thing that we often don't even really stop to think *why* diversification is so critical to a well-built financial plan. But the reason is simple: Diversification helps create a balance between safety and maximized potential gains. Economies change, markets transform, and strategies must adapt. When they don't, the outcomes are predictable but not often pleasant. Today, a seismic shift is occurring in the supply demand fundamentals of our economy. As a retiree or pre-retiree, building a foundation under your money may end up being one of the more profitable decisions you can make.

Losses are inevitable and expected in the investment world. Brokers often soothe investors who are upset with worn out platitudes like: "don't panic, you're in it for the long run," "stay the course," and "don't lock in your losses by selling now," "the market always comes back." Many of these ideas are designed to handle "Nervous Nellies" who call brokers wondering what happened to their money. Many of these principles may work fine in the contribution and accumulation phase of a person's life, but can be disastrous in the withdrawal phase.

Most importantly, don't **"Diversify Under Misguided Beliefs!"**

CHAPTER 8

IN RETIREMENT, MISTAKES ARE MEASURED IN DOLLARS, NOT PERCENTS

IN 2000 THE S&P 500 ONLY LOST 11 PERCENT. An 11 percent loss for a 37 year old division manager investing in a $200,000 retirement account is not only a yawn, but an opportunity to buy more of the same investments. It's called Dollar Cost Averaging (DCU). A 10 percent loss for a 67 year old retired engineer living on a $400,000 portfolio is quite a different matter. If he needs $20,000 annual withdrawals from the portfolio to sustain his lifestyle, a 10 percent loss means his family is short the investment loss plus the $20,000 withdrawn for family income. The 67 year old engineer won't want to hear about "buying more on the dips" after losing $60,000. It's a different math problem.

To a retiree, the cost of every mistake is measured in spendable dollars, not in "percents." The younger investor can afford to think in percents. He is not turning the money into spendable cash. The retired investor is buying milk, food, gas, and a lifestyle in real time.

Let's explore: If you start with $400,000 and make 9 percent, you've increased your net worth by by $36,000. You can easily withdraw 4 percent or 5 percent. That's easy math. It's also only one year in a sequence of 25 to 35 more years. All of us know—experts included—that there is no idea what fate markets will experience from year to year. Only a true clairvoyant can tell you where the markets will be one year from today. If you run into a few years like 2000-2002, you can see how someone can unexpectedly find themselves in a poor predicament. Because all of us are human, we become anchored in beliefs. That can be a dangerous thing for investors. We get a sense of comfort from familiarity. From 1995 to 1999, many investors doubled - and some even tripled -their net worth in the stock market, as the greatest consecutive gains in the history of stocks were recorded:

1995	37.58
1996	22.96
1997	33.36
1998	28.58
1999	21.04

From December 31, 1995 to December 31, 1999, investors who held the stocks comprising the S & P 500 enjoyed a 28.7% average annual return—the greatest uninterrupted sequence of returns in stock market history

It's not difficult to see how everyday investors could become used to these kinds of returns. In fact, they became anchored in their belief systems. Their sense of confidence, comfort, and even wealth, caused many of them to retire early or to confirm their plan to retire in 1999 and 2000, prior to the collapse of the NASDAQ and the natural reversion to the mean that began later in 2000. Many felt no need to make a change in strategy.

Summary: Base Your Retirement Income

On Math, Not Markets

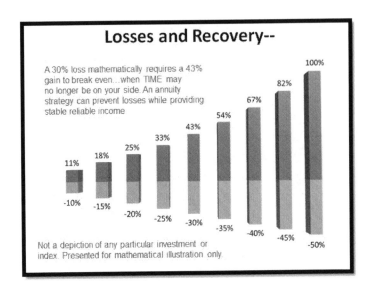

A 30% Loss Requires a 43% Gain To Break Even, A 50 percent Loss Requires a 100% Gain to Break Even.

Markets may defy gravity at times but reversion to the mean is a mathematical principal you must never ignore, in fact you can't. You won't have to look for it, it will find you. What goes up always comes down, and once your principal is down (also known as "capital impairment" in financial planning circles), you are totally reliant on market outcomes and will need to stop withdrawals if you want to see a recovery of your money. That's really not practical in retirement. You need income. Withdrawals and fees deepen your losses and slice off your gains. To a 37 year old investor, a 10 percent, 11 percent or 20 percent loss is a buying opportunity. To the already retired investor with $400,000, a 20 percent loss is $80,000 out the window. **Because the loss and withdrawal affects the principal so dramatically, a much larger gain is required to bring the account back to even.**

Retirement "Don't"—Don't Play Fast and Loose With Your Retirement – Someone is *Always* Faster

In the accumulation phase, you could afford to have been off a bit in your calculations. The goal was to be eighty percent correct rather than a hundred percent wrong. It even worked out that way sometimes!

In the decumulation phase, you are making decisions today that could have a deep impact on your future many years from now. Once a mistake is made and money is gone, it's gone. Being a few percent off today, can lead to being 20 percent short 20 years from now.

Airline pilots use GPS systems to set their course prior to take off. If you are flying from Los Angeles to New York, a 3,000 mile trip, being one percent off while in LA can literally land you closer to Buffalo or southern New Jersey.

Mutual funds and ETFs are built for the accumulation phase; Annuities are built specifically for the de-cumulation phase

Mutual funds and ETFs are for working people adding regularly to their portfolios. They are not built as storage tanks for retirement money. Their value changes every day at the market close. ETFs change their value according to markets from minute to minute. You might think you are pretty fast at getting out of the market in a downturn because you own a computer and can be looking at your account within minutes. Even Jesse James ran into a faster hand, but you are up against supercomputers and logarithms.

Today's stock market is dominated by High Frequency Traders and program trading. I'm not exaggerating when I say that information you receive that is a few minutes old is no longer news. Nearly a trillion dollars a day changes hands in the New York Stock Exchange alone. High Frequency Trading (HFT) has spread to global markets as well. Many are trying to outlaw it in England.

Clearly, a retired person, even one with a fast hand, a fast computer, and an IQ of 180, should have a significant amount of capital out of harm's way. That being said, large amounts of money sitting at zero percent in the bank is not out of harm's way. Inflation will kill you.

Parts of your plan must be precise and specific. You can wing it and speculate with a portion of your money, but it must not be your future income money. Mistakes are too easy to make and too difficult to correct. You've come too far to make mistakes now.

<u>The Goal: No More Income Worries, No Matter What: Why carefully selected annuities can't be beat for lifelong income.</u>

With a hybrid index annuity, the saga above would not have occurred for the 67 year old engineer. The $16,000 a year would be paid for both his and his wife's lifetimes regardless of capitulations in the market. No income worries, no matter what.

You wouldn't go a day without insuring your family home. In turbulent times like these, you shouldn't consider going a day without income insurance either (and it costs far less than home owners insurance). Annuities buy future income at 25 percent to 40 percent discounts.

The reason so many retiring professionals are rolling over their 401(k)'s and 403b's into Hybrid Index annuity accounts is for the certainty—a "concrete" floor under their lifetime savings. They want the assurance that they can get out *all the money out that they put in* and be assured of one or two lifetime incomes from the account from an insurance company. No Wall Street brokerage account can offer that. Wall Street investments can eat money once withdrawals begin, and you still have to pay. Annuities pay you money so you can eat, and are built for sustainable withdrawals. Which one makes more sense in retirement?

The Hybrid index annuity may occasionally provide intriguing returns, but it is an income and preservation tool first and foremost. The true value is seen when markets are falling and others are losing capital. With the annuity strategy, your money is safe, and your future income is secure. You can sleep at night knowing your money will keep coming your way, no matter what happens in the markets.

The reason so many retiring professionals are rolling over their 401(k)'s and 403b's into Hybrid Index annuity accounts is for the *certainty*—a "concrete" floor under their lifetime savings. They want the assurance that they can get out *all the money out that they put in* and be assured of one or two lifetime incomes from the account from an insurance company. No Wall Street brokerage account can offer that.

CHAPTER 9

WHY YOU CAN'T GET OUT OF YOUR OWN WAY WHEN INVESTING

AMERICANS TODAY ARE ASKED TO MAKE HUNDREDS of financial decisions in the course of a year. Many of them are little ones and have only a short term consequence. Then there are the *big ones* with long term consequences. Undoubtedly, the decision about where to place your savings to pay yourself a sustainable income that will last 30 or 40 years is the biggest.

It's not only a huge decision; it's a moving, 1000 piece puzzle. The markets, the economy, the national debt, the Eurozone crisis, the Middle East, your future health, currency wars, inflation, kids, grandkids, mom, dad - the list is endless. It's a situation that is bound to make retirees a little tense – a little emotional.

Emotions get in the way of great money management because they lead to subconscious bias. Psychologists have identified three kinds of biases that affect our decisions:

- **Cognitive Bias:** Decisions we make because of a lack of understanding.
- **Emotional Bias:** Decisions we make because of our emotional makeup.
- **Social Bias:** Decisions we make based on how we see ourselves in the world.

These biases are survival instincts—they are shortcuts in thinking that can save your life in the jungle, but can cause errors in statistical judgment and definitely can cost you money on Wall Street.

How Emotions Play in the Market

"Cognitive dissonance" is one of the most well-known types of cognitive biases. Cognitive dissonance is very common, and just about everyone has experienced it at least once in their lives. It is the feeling of tension or anxiety caused by holding two opposing beliefs or thoughts at the same time. Investors are overrun by cognitive dissonance because there are so many credible sounding and opposing opinions coming from so many news sources, 24/7/365.

"Illusory correlation" is another one of the more commonly known types of cognitive biases. It is very common in investing. Illusory correlation describes a situation where someone perceives a correlation, or relationship between two variables, when in reality, there is little or no relationship between the variables. One example that cost many investors money was the correlation between technology stocks in the 1990s and guaranteed profits.

"Hot cognition" is a new type of bias based on the mood of the person making decisions. Someone in a heightened state of emotion, such as anger, fear, and even joy, can make errors in judgment based on his or her emotional state. In the case of hot cognition, a person may make a decision too quickly, without the proper amount of reflection.

"Cold cognition" is also a relatively new type of cognitive bias. It is the complementary cognitive bias of hot cognition. Just as hot cognition describes decision making affected by heightened emotional states, cold cognition occurs when a person makes a decision while experiencing very little emotion. This type of low-energy and attention decision-making is also problematic. Instead of making decisions too fast and while emotionally charged, a person experiencing cold cognition makes decisions based on little reflection because of lack of interest.

Two other forms of cognitive bias can make an investor stay put and freeze, even when losing money, and even when the markets are clearly overvalued as they were in 1999 and 2007:

Status-Quo Bias: We humans tend to be apprehensive of change, which often leads us to make choices that guarantee that things remain the same, or change as little as possible.

Gambler's Fallacy: We tend to put a tremendous amount of weight on previous events, believing that they'll somehow influence future outcomes. The classic example is coin-tossing. After flipping heads, say, five consecutive times, our inclination is to predict an increase in likelihood that the next coin toss will be tails. But in reality, the odds are still 50/50. As statisticians say, the outcomes in different tosses are *statistically independent* and the probability of any outcome is still 50 percent.

Sunk Cost Bias: The refusal to leave a bad situation because an investment in time or money has already been made.

Bandwagon effect: The tendency to do or believe what others do or believe.

It turns out, our friend Frank from the first chapter was in a state of mental fatigue caused by 12 years of dealing with virtually all of the above. To use the 50-dollar word, Frank was stuck in an "illusory correlation" believing that money in the market was the same as money in the bank or in an annuity. He felt like the stock market could go up any time which would fix his sunk cost feelings of regret. He was anchored in beliefs that caused him to consider that "stocks always make 10 percent" and stocks "always come back" after a fall. He also saw so many other people in the stock market, believing that they must know what they are doing, that he was caught up in the Bandwagon effect. Simply put, he got used to the "old normal."

Will investors ever return to the heydays of the 1990s and recoup the money they lost over the past twelve years? They may recoup the dollars, but they will never recoup the time. The economy is not turning out the new innovation that drove the '80s and '90s. And, the markets are not mathematically aligned for a new wave of growth without traveling into bubble territory, which would place investors back in the position of having to overcome the gambler's fallacy, the sunk cost syndrome, and the bandwagon effect.

The new wave of retirees wants income plans that are specific, measurable, attainable, reliable and timely. That's the kind of planning that I specialize in. I leave the pie in the sky to others. I concentrate on money in your hand, money in the bank, and money coming your way in steady cash flow. It's also money that isn't directed by emotion, although retirees who have a steady, reliable income feel very, very happy. Especially in this economy.

How to "You-Proof" Your Retirement and Secure the Safety of Your Retirement Income: Choose a Hybrid Annuity for All, or Part, of Your Rollover

Homes don't burn down very often, but people are outliving their incomes more and more. Why is it that people insure their homes as a matter of course, but fail to insure their own money? They are not insuring their incomes while their investments are fully intact at younger ages, choosing instead to rely on market returns and bank rates to live on. They are simply choosing the wrong tools for the job.

They are diversified – but they rely on misguided beliefs and withdraw level amounts of money from fluctuating accounts. Remember: Diversification *spreads* risk, it doesn't eliminate it. Another byproduct of diversification is a lower overall yield.

In order to be truly diversified, especially when in or near retirement, a retiree needs to have a significant portion of assets in "non-correlated" alternative holdings. In other words, they need an asset that is invulnerable to stock market volatility and impervious to systematic risk (the whole system falling at once like it did in 2008).

Getting the most out of each dollar with an IRA or 401(k) rollover is everyone's goal. When the key risks in retirement can be avoided or reduced, while delivering a permanent contractual income at the same rates bonds once paid – fixed index annuities start to look very good.

Annuities can readily be used for an IRA or 401(k) rollover. In fact, that could end up being one of the smartest moves you ever make. Why? With the right annuity, your income has a basis of insurance protection. All forms of annuities can be used for an IRA or 401(k), and the annuity contract provides you with a guarantee that you will always have income, virtually identical to a pension.

Retirement "Do"--

Getting the most out of each dollar with an IRA or 401(k) rollover is everyone's goal. When the key risks in retirement (sequence of returns risk, longevity risk, interest rate risk) can be avoided or reduced, while delivering a permanent contractual income at the same rates bonds once paid – fixed index annuities start to look very good.

Contrary to popular misconception, annuities are wise choices for a 401(k) or 403b rollover, especially when using Next Generation Index annuities. Imagine: an asset with no fees for administration, or investment management. Moderate growth with principal safety and no fees, combined with a pension-like income benefit. Ample liquidity, and protection from bear markets. Anything on that list that you find to be a negative? Remember, all or part of your rollover can be dedicated to the annuity, depending on suitability, age, and goals.

Some Annuity Tips:

Annuities are part investment, part insurance. They are designed as a tool for retirement and best suited for people age 45 to 79. Not all annuities are alike, so make sure you are comparing "apples to apples" and getting impartial information.

Key point: Beware of the fees of variable annuities. Newer forms of annuities, referred to as "Next Generation" fixed index annuities offer a combination of principal protection, moderate participation in the upside of market indexes with no market losses, and lifetime income without the need for "annuitizing."

1) An annuity is only one of <u>many</u> tools for building a retirement portfolio—choose wisely. An annuity is not the only building block in your financial plan. You will want to keep a balance. Your other investments will work together with the annuity to help you stay true to your risk tolerance and time-horizon needs.

2) You do not choose an annuity to "replace" all stocks, bonds, or ETFs. A well-balanced portfolio is a combination of cash, income, and growth investments. A properly selected annuity is primarily a fixed income asset. The role it plays in a well planned retirement is that it can protect your principal, share in some of the markets' upside without taking market losses, and pay you a contractually guaranteed income for life without the need to "annuitize."

3) Know the four basic categories of annuities before you start comparing. There are four main categories of annuities: a) immediate b) variable c) fixed d) fixed index. You need to know the basics of each so that you can compare "apples to apples."

4) Caution: Annuity "haters" are simply trying to sell you something else. If you you've been on the web exploring annuities, you will find both lovers and haters. Remember the purpose of your money. Annuities are for preservation & income.

CHAPTER 10

WHAT THE "GURUS" GET WRONG ABOUT RETIREMENT

IF YOU ARE PIE-CHART PLANNING (I hope not), you may be relying on popular, main-stream financial advisors who are attempting to give advice to large groups of people. They mean well. Their hearts are in the right place. But they are not retirement planners. Take for example Suze Orman and Dave Ramsey. They have huge audiences, and thus cannot possibly give accurate advice to each person who listens to them because each person has a unique situation—age, income, savings. Suze and Dave give their best advice when it comes to younger people heavily in debt. They are very good at helping people see the wisdom of becoming debt-free. It is a worthy goal, but only one part of becoming financially independent.

Dave Ramsey and I share the Christian faith, and we both have a mission for helping people to achieve financial peace, but I could never use his mutual fund strategies in good conscience for people who are retiring with thirty to forty years of retirement ahead of them and very little certainty in markets, economies, and the Social Security system.

Suze Orman and Dave Ramsey are not driven by giving the best information tailored to each person. Rather, they are forced by the constraints of time and making "good television" to give broad brushstroke advice that pertains to the majority of their viewers.

And who is viewing? Well, Orman's biggest audience is the 25-42 year old category, with one of the largest demographics being 27 year old males. Ramsey also appeals to about the same age-range, with a large demographic being young adults who are trying to get out of debt and get a grip on being financially independent. Virtually all of the information presented by Orman and Ramsey is about *accumulating* wealth – not living off it in retirement.

For the person already out of debt, who has a paid off their house and has no credit cards outstanding, who is already retired, already over the age of 59 ½, and looking to withdraw from, rather than contribute to, their retirement accounts, of what value is advice about accumulating money in the markets? If your thought is "not much," you and I are on the same page. If it's not, it's time to change your thinking.

I'm not saying Orman and Ramsey aren't popular for a reason. They both have fans in older categories because they are entertaining and engaging – dare I say they are charismatic. They both preach good, solid, sensible values which we all have a craving for, regardless of age. I personally like both of them. Professionally, I think their advice can be toxic for many retirees and pre-retirees.

For example, how often do you hear a detailed discussion on either Orman's or Ramsey's shows about the Sequence of Returns Risk? How about the mathematical reality of Reverse Dollar Cost Averaging? These two concepts are the most important discussions for retirees who invest in market-reliant and interest-sensitive instruments like ETFs, mutual funds, and stocks. And they're being overlooked by these "gurus."

So, because of the audience that Orman and Ramsey entertain, it's safe to say their pie-charts are designed for a successful 30-year-old who is trying to accumulate wealth. And the successful pie chart for a 30-year-old would be a disaster for a 60-year-old, looking to start withdrawing money for income to support both basic living needs and an active lifestyle.

Orman and Ramsey both seem to support and promote a market-reliant, long-term crapshoot in the U.S. economy. Further, they seem to support the market of stocks, which is now dominated by high frequency traders, hedge fund managers, day traders, and those looking to short the market, not stay long. This is not wise investing for the retiree, and I shudder to think of retirees focusing their assets there. My advice: be careful taking their advice. Get a second opinion.

The Retirement Factor: What Can Go Wrong With Conventional Pie Chart Financial Planning—Really Wrong

> **"Investors should be skeptical of history-based models. Constructed by a nerdy-sounding priesthood using esoteric terms such as beta, gamma, sigma and the like, these models tend to look impressive. Too often, though, investors forget to examine the assumptions behind the models.**
>
> **Beware of geeks bearing formulas."**
>
> — *Warren Buffett*

Diversified pie charts organize investments into categories with easy to understand color-coding. The pie charts take the viewer from the micro view (little picture) to the macro view (big picture).

Here's what happens in "pie-chart land": investors look for a simplified macro view—the big picture—that "confirms" that they are making all the right moves with their investment strategies. How do they decide they're making the right moves? By listening to CNBC, Bloomberg and Fox; by going online to Vanguard, Fidelity, and Schwab; and by putting it all together, making sure their pie charts match the model pie charts of these information sources. Once that task is complete, they go back to "tweaking" and "improving" the micro view—the little picture—and looking for news that confirms their decisions. Hey, even the smartest among us do it—it's called Confirmation Bias.

Remember, Confirmation Bias is the tendency all people have to look for information that confirms what they want to believe. It is a survival instinct that can save your life in an emergency. When it comes to money, you have an honest and healthy desire to understand and process the avalanche of data coming at you 24/7 on cable TV and the internet. To make sense of it, you have to sort. In order to sort, you look for that which you recognize. Unfortunately, that which you recognize may not always be in your best interest, or may apply more aptly to a different point of time in your investment career.

When you're caught up in the Confirmation Bias, you're not making smart decisions. Instead, you are simply looking for information that affirms what you already think. So when you're constantly turning to the same sources offering the same advice, it can be hard to see if your investment strategy is working for you, or if you just want it to be because someone else says it could and should.

Micromanaging plus confirmation bias, plus pie-charting equals: a dangerous combination.

Times Have Changed; Retirement Investing Needs To, Too

As a retiree, you might have something to say to Suze Orman, Dave Ramsey, and Clark Howard right about now: *This ain't your grandfather's stock market and this ain't the 1980s.*

If I were going to look for a parallel in another time in history, it wouldn't be 1983 - the beginning of the glorious period of cyber innovation and stock market growth. The parallel I see is more like 1966, when our nation was looking for an end to overseas military conflict and the economy was beginning to slow down. Sound familiar? The year 1966 marked the beginning of the "Great Society" concept when social programs, fighting wars, and trying to get an economy going were matched up with a stock market that had hit and continued to flirt with market highs. Faith in the stock market had reached an apex for that time period.

What's so different about then and now? The big difference today is that we are on the other side of the hill from all the innovation that drove employment, wealth creation, real estate growth, and stock market growth from the 1980s and '90s. We are also at a point where the entitlements created by the Great Society concepts have now reached in excess of $80 trillion in unfunded liabilities and going on $17 trillion in near term debt.

The other difference is that we are not necessarily headed for a big inflation a la the 1970s. There is growing evidence that we are hopelessly stuck in deflation. What we have today is a high-tech Fed using digital dollars to commandeer a balance between monetary inflation and economic deflation. We have a society that has manufacturing capability but in which more of the production work is being done by fewer and fewer people. We have the highest paid robots in the world, but people are being asked to believe that their 401(k)'s will rise as the robots continue to turn out widgets. I hate to break it to you, but that probably won't happen.

While most people look at the Fed's money printing and think "This HAS to lead to inflation!" they are losing track of the number of Americans—Generation X and Y—that are actually out of work and doing service jobs in the hospitality, delivery, and food service industries rather than engineering and construction. These generations don't have big enough paychecks to get themselves out of debt, on their feet, raising families, sending their kids to college on their own dimes, building an investment portfolio for retirement, and then paying themselves an income that will last themselves and their spouses a lifetime.

Here's what happening: Generations X and Y (also known as Orman, Ramsey and Howard's viewerships) are stuck in jobs, not careers. The Baby Boomers and the Silent Generation told their kids they could be anything they wanted to be. Then we went into a recession and careers became an idle dream for Gen X and Y, making inflation hard to come by.

As the Baby Boomers and Silent Generation scale back on consumption and speculating in markets, and Gen X and Y stay waiting for work, the real economy is sliding. Ben Bernanke is doing his best to halt the slide. He is dropping $80 billion a month into the economy in newly created digital dollars--$960 billion a year (let's round it to a trillion) and all that can result is a stock market that is positive but not setting records. What if he stops? You don't want to know that answer if you have your nest egg tied up in market-reliant holdings.

Noted economist, *Forbes* contributor and Stanford PhD. Gary Schilling describes the current financial situation like this:

> *"In free markets, inflation results when demand exceeds supply, and deflation when supply exceeds demand, while prices are allowed to move up or down to bring supply and demand together. Historically inflation is associated with wartime because it's then that the federal government creates excess demand for goods and services on top of an already fully employed economy. ...The federal government is the only sector that can overspend enough to create inflation because it's the only with the credibility in financial markets to float the immense borrowing need to finance it...I don't believe that inflation is a monetary phenomenon (because the money supply can't be precisely defined and is too fluid to measure both in the increase and decrease.) Be careful what you wish for..."*

The wish list seen in polls generally includes:

- A cutback or elimination of wars and the military,
- More taxes on the wealthy,
- Increases in social security and healthcare benefits, with no means testing,
- A rise in interest rates on bonds and bank accounts.

The above list would be a financial disaster of immense proportions. If you believe these things are coming, then you may sincerely want to do more "tweaking" of your portfolio to include less reliance on stock and bond ETFs, and more reliance on insured products like annuities. Don't be afraid of annuities! Yes, there are annuities I wouldn't recommend. In fact, I reject over 98% of all annuities on the market. But the 2% you are hearing about or learning about could be keeping you from feeling more secure about your future. Take the time to learn more from a fiduciary advisor. As a Certified Annuity Specialist® with over 20 years in the business, I take pride in helping clients get over their preconceived notions about annuities. When properly used, annuities can be your secret weapon for not only surviving but thriving in the years ahead.

Many people also wish for higher interest rates on bonds and CDs, yet it would be devastating to the economy and would have a negative effect on both the stock market (investors leaving the risk for higher safe rates) and the bond market (those who stayed around in "conservative" fixed income ETFS and funds would see a crushing blow to their accumulated values).

In the past, if financial analysts pointed to the value and wisdom of annuities, many would have looked at them as members of the Flat Earth Society. Today, the annuity principle is coming into focus.

> In the past, if financial analysts pointed to the value and wisdom of annuities, many would have looked at them as members of the Flat Earth Society. In the future, *not* owning an annuity in your portfolio may qualify for a lifetime membership.

CHAPTER 11

YOUR RETIREMENT PUZZLE IS MISSING A PIECE

AN INCREASING NUMBER OF RETIREES will spend three or even four decades in retirement. Some of these retirees, primarily those with pensions, will spend their last years financially secure, able to concentrate their time on family, friends, new experiences, personal growth, and the planning of their legacies.

Others will not.

For most retirees, their retirement years will hinge on the uncertainties of market outcomes, and their time spent on budgeting around fluctuating income. Yes, retirees need to take the money for their expenses off the stock market table – but even that isn't quite enough to ensure a stable, reliable income. There's a missing piece, but let's look at the rest of the puzzle first.

The Retirement Puzzle Has 3 Main Pieces – And They're Not As Reliable As You Think

1. **Social Security** - Most retirees rely heavily upon Social Security and related government programs. Social Security, which provides, on average, about 40 percent of retirement income, will face increasing financial pressure in the coming years as more Baby Boomers reach retirement age. The ratio of people in their retirement years (65 and older) compared to those in their working years (20 to 64) will rise from 20.6 percent in 2005 to 35 percent in 2030, according to the Census Bureau. **The system will strain to pay the benefits of current retirees, and may be combined with huge projected deficits, increasing Medicare, Medicaid and health care costs, and exploding debt.** A recent report from the Congressional

Budget Office shows that for the first time in 25 years, Social Security is now collecting less in taxes than it is spending on benefits. For these reasons, Americans are understandably nervous about the prospects of Social Security over the long haul.

2. **Traditional Pensions** - With a traditional pension, saving and investing are done by employers, and these employers bear the risk that retirement assets will fall short of promised benefits. However, the self-managed pensions are in trouble, by and large. According to the most recent numbers from the Employee Benefit Research Institute, the number of workers covered by traditional pensions has declined dramatically and continues to decline. Moreover, a growing number of the remaining company pensions are in the hands of the Pension Benefit Guaranty Corp., a government agency and payer of last resort when pension funds go under. **The PBGC is underfunded by billions of dollars.**

3. **Home Equity** - A sure sign of the "new normal" is the lack of confidence in the value of one's own home. In the past, home equity was on par with money in the bank. There was the notion that no one can lose money on their own home, and for many people, their residence was a vitally important retirement asset. However, history reveals that most of us should not have been so reliant on home equity for a sense of lasting wealth. Yale economist Robert Shiller compared home prices since 1890 and found that except for two spectacular booms – the first after World War II and the second starting in 1998 – real estate appreciation has been unimpressive after figuring in inflation. **Now that the housing bubble has burst and home values have plummeted, consumer confidence has been shaken to its foundations.** While some may use reverse mortgages to extract equity from their homes in retirement, most people are uncomfortable with the concept and banks

are finding it non-profitable. The top three banks doing reverse mortgages three years ago have left the industry. The lesson: Lasting wealth comes from sources of sustainable income, not from stagnant assets.

Concerns and problems with these traditional retirement anchors mean that more retirees and near-retirees will need to rely upon their personal savings to get by – whether in defined contribution plans such as 401(k)s and IRAs - or in other available savings alternatives. Based upon a variety of sources, including the National Retirement Risk Index, calculated by the Center for Retirement Research at Boston College, it is clear that we are not saving nearly enough for retirement. Indeed, a record 51 percent of U.S. households are now considered at risk of not having enough money to sustain their standard of living for their entire lifetimes.

A recent Wells Fargo Retirement Fitness Survey found that those 50-59 years of age expect to spend 10 percent of their assets per year in retirement. The figure was arrived at by asking respondents how much they currently earned at work, how much they expected their investments to make, both up to and during retirement, and how much they planned to spend on an annual basis. The respondents expected their savings to grow by 8.7 percent per year, an amount that is double the average rate of return over the past 25 years by American investors, according to Dalbar Inc. (www.Dalbar.com)

There is hope, however.

A study prepared by Ernst & Young on behalf of the non-profit Americans for Secure Retirement entitled *Retirement Vulnerability of New Retirees* has found that those with guaranteed retirement income beyond Social Security, such as income annuities, are much better prepared for retirement. It also found that middle-income Americans entering retirement without a guaranteed source of income beyond Social Security, such as an annuity, will, on average, have to reduce their standard of living by 32 percent to minimize (but not guarantee) the likelihood of outliving their assets. This reduction will be necessary even if assuming that retirees can maintain the same standard of living with income equal to only 59-71 percent of their pre-retirement wages.

> **"Sixty-five percent of U.S. households are now at risk of not having enough money to sustain their standard of living in retirement."**
>
> —The Center for Retirement Research at Boston College

While we are focused on pre-retirees and retirees, the study also found that the next wave of retirees (3-8 years from now) will have an even higher risk of outliving their financial assets than those currently at retirement age.

That's why income annuities are so vital. As the Ernst & Young report states and other academic research confirms:

"Without additional guaranteed lifetime income streams, such as income provided by an annuity, middle-income Americans are at high risk of outliving their financial assets and living their final years in poverty."

CHAPTER 12

ANNUITIES MADE SIMPLE

Why Annuities?

LET'S START WITH WHAT BROKERAGE HOUSES don't want you to know. There is much more to annuities than "variable" or "immediate" – in fact, the new generation of annuities includes some of the best options for creating safe, sustainable lifetime income that isn't dependent on market performance. When you take the time to understand that an annuity is meant to provide income stability for your portfolio, rather than a way to outperform the stock market, you're on your way to understanding why an annuity belongs in your portfolio.

> **"An annuity and an investment are really two different things. You don't buy an annuity just to make money. You buy it to make sure that when you are 97 years old you have an income coming in."**
>
> *– Professor Olivia S. Mitchell, Wharton School of Business, "How Much Money Will You Need for Retirement?" August 2003.*

The Need for a Guaranteed Lifetime Income Has Never Been Greater

Most Americans are on a path to income depletion and potential financial ruin – that's not my opinion; that is the conclusion of numerous studies by Ernst & Young, the Wharton School of Business, Boston College, Boston University, the University of Illinois and other academic and professional researchers. This frightening fate isn't reserved for the less fortunate *many*; the fortunate *few* are also on a glide-path to lifestyle decline if they remain loyal to investment strategies that aren't adapted to coming trends.

> **Two things have changed over the last 10 years:**
>
> 1) The **world,** and 2) **you.** You are not the risk taker
>
> you were back then and the world itself, is riskier.
>
> The facts have changed. And when the facts change, smart people change. If the path you are currently on was leading you to financial shortfall, how soon would you want to know?

A steady stream of guaranteed income in retirement reduces the risk that you will outlive your savings or face significant reductions to your standard of living. Without solid and steady gains, the typical spending habits of an affluent couple could run headlong into flat markets, unexpected global events, poorly-timed health setbacks, and kids moving back home after job loss or divorce. If the spending levels aren't adjusted downward, and if interest rates don't rise up to meet expenses, this financially catastrophic but plausible combination can quite easily lead to poverty in 15 to 20 years. Whether a family with a million goes through $100,000 a year without gaining anything on their investments, or a person with $100,000 in assets spends $10,000 a year, the outcome is the same: Financial Ruin in as little as 15 years or less.

Add inflation, long-term healthcare needs, and a good long life to this equation, and you'll really find yourself in trouble. The Wall Street advice of dialing up the risk to meet future needs is suddenly not resonating as it once did. People with common sense, who have bounced around this volatile market already, understand that the market is a 50/50 proposition with no guarantees. Taking on more risk may simply lead to deeper losses, not retirement bliss.

But what about those guaranteed sources of income – the traditional defined-benefit pension plans and Social Security? Both offer the investor an income stream for life during retirement, and they worked very well for our parents and grandparents. Unfortunately, few of us retiring now have a pension. We have a 401(k) or an IRA, which means that the responsibility to provide a lifetime income stream during retirement has been transferred from employers – to you. Statistical research indicates most Americans aren't handling that responsibility well.

The secret to success is knowledge: knowing your options, comparing annuities, and including the right mix of investments in your portfolio. Since there are so many misconceptions about annuities – mostly generated by the media which, frankly, isn't well informed on the subject – let's start with the basics.

> **"An investment in knowledge pays the most dividends."**
>
> *-Benjamin Franklin, who purchased annuities for the cities of Boston and Philadelphia - which lasted more than 200 years.*

What is an annuity?

An Annuity is a unique type of financial account, issued by state regulated insurance companies, which can provide safety, tax deferral, principal guarantees, and a secure retirement income for life. Hybrid annuities combine some of the best features of fixed and variable annuities, which is why their demand is on the rise.

The ultimate advantage of an annuity over an investment or savings account is the reserve-backed guarantee that you will never outlive your income.

You have a floor under your money.

Placing money into an annuity is safer than making almost any kind of investment. In fact, annuities are the only form of financial asset that are backed by matching reserves (and surplus reserves) in a stable, regulated portfolio that is required to be managed conservatively by state law.

And, an insurance company offering annuities in 50 states has 50 regulators monitoring its practices.

Perhaps this is one reason why the safety record is so good. Your money is backed by the claims paying ability of the insurer, who must follow statutory guidelines for conservative risk management. This is a financial promise that has a long, solid track record.

The 4 Types of Annuities You Need to Know

When you begin your research into annuities, you'll come across terms like "fixed," "variable," "indexed," "immediate," and "deferred." You may also hear terms like "cap," "spread," "income rider," or "premium bonus." Don't let the industry jargon throw you; here's what you need to know.

The Four Main Kinds of Annuities are:

1. **Immediate** – Best for pure income, no access to the lump sum.

2. **Fixed** – Works like a bank CD, with guarantees of principal protection and income.

3. **Variable** – Invested directly into the market, no protection of principal, often contains hidden fees.

4. **Hybrid** – Also known as a Fixed Index annuity, the term "hybrid" comes from taking the fixed annuity's principal protection with the ability to grow with the upside potential of the market. Key difference from a variable: Your money is never invested directly into the stock market, so if the stock market dips, your principal remains untouched. If the stock market rises, your principal will grow with it.

Annuity differences: A Quick Overview

The real difference between the four annuity types is *how much control you maintain over your principal values.*

A fixed or hybrid annuity can be an alternative to a bond or bank CD—a time instrument that gives you a full return of your money on a certain date that you select, plus a reasonable return on your money. Neither fixed nor hybrid annuities are designed to hit it out of the park from an aggressive growth standpoint, so don't go looking to outperform the stock market. Do go with a fixed or hybrid annuity to enjoy the satisfaction and peace of having a commitment from a hundred year old, multi-billion dollar insurer to guard your money and pay you a steady reliable income for as long as you want.

Did You Know?

- Annuities date back to the days of Rome: Historical records show Julius Caesar awarded them to gladiators and to wives of fallen gladiators.

- Detailed records of annuities first appeared in published form as early as 1483.

- Annuities were made a part of our tax code by the Tax Reform Act of 1913 and fall under similar rules to IRAs.

- Babe Ruth used annuities to avoid the risk of the stock market and thus survived and thrived in the Great Depression.

- No one has EVER lost a penny to the stock market in a hybrid index annuity. Not ever.

- Variable annuities are sold on the concept of "unlimited upside;" however the effects of market losses and compounding fees can result in poor performance relative to the market.

So You Have an IRA Rollover Decision – Now What?

Annuities are surprisingly flexible; they allow you to accumulate retirement savings within an IRA or on a tax-deferred basis outside of an IRA. In five, seven, or ten years, you can reap the benefits of your savings in a lump sum payment, similar to a bond. In fact, many planners are turning to annuities to provide a replacement for the bond component in laddered income plans. Bonds can no longer be used for laddering, and bond mutual funds lack safety of principal. Annuities are quickly growing up to take over the bond market. In fact, Annuities are fast becoming the number-one option for 401(k), 403(b) and IRA rollovers as well, as retiring professionals increasingly seek safer havens for their hard-earned savings.

Choosing the Right Annuity for the Long Haul

Annuities are 250 pound linebackers when it comes to creating permanent income – they are built for the job. Today's top insurance companies (the only ones I recommend) have been around longer than most of today's retirees, paying steady income and never missing a payment through wars, depressions, terror attacks, and "Black Swans" (impossible to predict financial pitfalls). However, it's important to choose the correct annuity for your financial situation, one which works in harmony with the rest of your portfolio. Not all annuity models and features are available in all states, so always work with a licensed, ethical annuity adviser.

As an important first step, visit www.MyAnnuityGuy.com™ to receive a free copy of *The Proper Use Of An Annuity In A Retirement Income Portfolio*, available by mail or immediate download. This guide will help you learn how an annuity may be a fit for you, in plain English*.

Note: An annuity is a long term financial vehicle designed for income purposes, whether on a deferred or immediate basis. Not all products are available in all states, and while most annuities do not have upfront fees, they often carry potential surrender charges for early withdrawal. See contract for details. Withdrawals prior to age 59 ½ may incur tax penalties.* I favor plain English explanations, however, we live in a world of tight regulations. For further technical reference, view the National Association of Insurance Commissioner's Buyers Guide to Fixed Annuities. For a referral to a licensed agent, call (888)369-5757

The L.U.C.K Test

Annuity IQ	L Liquidity Access to principal values at inception. Provisions for penalty-free withdrawals for liquidity over time	U Utility Contractually guaranteed pensionized income for life, either as a permanent feature or through a rider at a higher rate than typically found in bonds.	C Control Multiple Flexible financial options, in addition to a pensionized sustainable income.	K Knowledge Knowing that my principal values are 100% accounted for, 100% of my money goes to work right away with no sales charges deducted. My money is safe, accessible, and not being hit with fees for administration, life insurance, subaccounts, etc. My principal values cannot decline due to market conditions. My beneficiaries can receive my remaining balance upon death with no surrender charges. ALL of the above are met.
Immediate Annuity	NO	YES	NO	NO
Fixed Annuity	YES	YES	YES	YES
Variable Annuity	YES	YES	YES	NO
Hybrid Index Annuity	YES	YES	YES	YES

This information is general in nature. No specific product is being promoted. Liquidity features vary among deferred annuities. See contract for details. Withdrawals prior to age 59 ½ may incur tax penalties from the IRS. Not all products available in all states. Guarantees rely on the claims paying ability of the insurer. Not a bank deposit. Not an offer to buy or sell a security. No information in this publication promotes any form of variable annuity or security. Variable annuities are complex instruments combining elements of insurance and securities. Read the prospectus and meet with a qualified adviser first.

Every annuity comes with the ability to make a lifetime income when you bring it home from the factory. It is simply a matter of tailoring your income needs to the right category of annuity. The choice will come down to when you take the income (if ever), how much you will receive, and whether or not you want to maintain liquid access to your lump sum principal.

Each type of annuity provides income in different ways or at different times—but income is the key reason to own an annuity or annuities.

You know by now that I don't always like rules of thumb, but...

Here are a few guidelines:

- If you aren't sure when you want income, your choice would be a deferred annuity.

- If you never want to risk your principal in the market, your choices would narrow down to a fixed index annuity (Hybrid) or a fixed (declared rate) annuity.

- Combination Hybrid annuities make that choice even more simple—you get your choice of declared rate or index all in one annuity account, or mix and match.

- An immediate annuity is pure income. It is basically an irrevocable decision and is the source of much of the information you hear about annuities being "illiquid." As in – your money is locked in. That isn't always bad if you simply want the most income bang for your buck and you have no other use for the money except income.

More on Immediate Annuities

I use immediate annuities in my annuity ladders when they are a fit. They act almost like a pension, allowing you to put in a lump sum to work immediately to generate maximum, safe cash flow. In exchange for a lump sum of capital, known in the insurance world as your "premium payment," you have a reserve-backed, actuarially calculated income for the rest of your life, just like a pension.

There's a hitch: At the time of this printing, rates of payout are historically low due to interest rates being low. However, the rates of payout are based more on your age than the interest rate. For example, while a 76 year old male may receive a 9.54 percent rate of payout from an A+ carrier, a 71 year old female may receive an 8.2 percent rate of payout. If they band together and take out an annuity on both their lives, the rate of payout from the same company drops to 6.2 percent.

Where's the logic? Simple: Women live longer than men, so the insurance company lowers the rate of payout in order to pay longer. Men statistically die sooner, so the insurance company is willing to pay more to an older male. This is actuarial science and is another reason why annuities have a powerful safety record. If this couple is married, you might think they have found the ideal plan. One problem: With these rates of payout, when the annuitant dies, the money is gone. They can get a joint immediate annuity, but actuarial science takes over and the result is a 6.2 percent payout - but covers both of them for life. You can also choose "period certain" provisions that protect beneficiaries for varying lengths of time. There are no fees for these, but simply a lower amount of income. The lack of liquidity combined with today's low interest rates makes immediate annuities the LEAST popular form of annuities, even though the income is the highest.

- A **fixed annuity** is similar to a CD but has a different purpose. You will get a fixed rate of income by agreeing to position your money in it for a fixed amount of time. With a fixed annuity your money will grow *tax-advantaged*, meaning you won't pay taxes on it while it's growing.

- A **variable annuity** is most similar to owning mutual funds and is also tax deferred, but your money is directly invested the market with no principal protection. Fees are charged every year, even when the market goes down. This means you can trade within your variable annuity, but you can lose if the market falls. In addition, you'll pay taxes when you take your money out if there are gains. If you are a more aggressive risk taker, you may feel comfortable with a plan like this. Most of the bad press on fees revolves around variable annuities.

- The **fixed indexed annuity is a hybrid** between a fixed and a variable annuity. There are no imposed annual fees or deductions. A fixed index annuity allows you to earn interest credits based on the upside movements of the market—but with no exposure to the downside. Your interest gains are captured automatically by contract, never to be lost again to the market; your account can move only forward, not backwards. Optionally, you can attach an income account or "rider" to a fixed index annuity that can grow your income value by as much as 8 percent annually, compounded.

With the Fixed Index Annuities (FIAs), there are no annual administration, subaccount, or life insurance fees and your principal is never reduced by sales charges, which means 100 percent of your money goes to work right away. By adding a withdrawal rider (that can be dropped later, but not added) you are in a fortified position of safety at a time in your life when that is of paramount importance. You are unaffected by market declines, and own the right - but not the obligation - to turn on and turn off a pensionized income that quietly and powerfully grows 24/7/365.

That said, I do not give a blanket recommendation to FIAs. In fact, I'll confess that I don't like about 98 percent of annuities out there. The 2 percent that meet key requirements, however, are exceptional. The ones that I do like are the foundations of many successful plans.

Should you put all your money into something like this? No. Should you put some of it in something like this? I'd give that a yes, based on the fact that it meets our needs for:

1. Safety of capital over time

2. Overall fee reduction

3. Dramatic risk reduction

4. Flexibility in our future income plan

5. A safeguard against inflation

6. Stability

7. Predictability

8. Ample liquidity

9. The ability to take the money and run or...

10. Annuitize at a later date, your choice.

If you choose to turn it into an immediate annuity ten years from now, for example, your rate stands to be significantly higher than that of a variable annuity or even an immediate annuity started now at your younger age. For these reasons and more, Hybrid annuities make a tailored fit within the IQ Wealth Smarter Bucketing System™.

Clearly, annuities come in many shapes and sizes. You can start an annuity with as little as $10,000 and many companies will accept annuity applications of up to $2.5 million.

Annuity Alert: Beware the "Free" Steak Dinner**...**

When you're invited to a "free" dinner seminar on annuities, or even click on a "free" website, you will eventually run into three types of agents:

...FIRST, is the agent who truly **believes he or she is doing a "good job,"** but sadly hasn't done enough research or is unqualified to give full financial advice. Their knowledge of hybrid index annuities is limited. They can be very nice, but are in over their heads.

...SECOND, is the agent who understands how most hybrid index annuities work, but **unfortunately cares more about commissions** and sales awards than finding the best payouts from the safest companies. Many of these agents decide on <u>their</u> favorite annuity rather than helping you compare. But they are great salespeople.

...THIRD, is the **more experienced agent whose "cheese" has been moved.** They have done little or no research on hybrid index annuities and therefore are unqualified to make statements in public about how they work. **But that won't stop them!** They remember the good old days of selling variable annuities and REITS and can't understand that Baby Boomers have moved on to a new math problem—prudent retirees have grown more conservative and now want more safety, less risk, and more control over their money. They want a plan for stable, sustained income, with layers of principal protection. They don't want to stand idly by while their principal is eroded by poor markets and ongoing fees.

Options, Extras & Upgrades

Unfortunately, many annuity buyers buy the first annuity they see, or are so un-impressed by what their local insurance salesman has to offer, that they never see today's most advanced annuities.

Some annuities offer guaranteed withdrawal rates of 5 percent to 7 percent for life – for both you and a spouse. You can even find annuities that will allow you to take 4 percent annual withdrawals indefinitely, and leave every penny of your principal to your beneficiaries.

The right kind of annuity can also provide other practical features. For example, you can make partial lump sum withdrawals along the way or take monthly income – with no surrender charges (contrary to media reports). An annuity also comes with the guarantee of a lifetime pension-like income. You can choose regular payments for a specified period of time (e.g., for five years, ten years) or choose a "paycheck for life," similar to a pension. This option is known as annuitizing, is generally irrevocable, and is not always a popular idea among retirees.

The annuity industry has responded to the demand for more flexibility and liquidity with income riders – which can be added to hybrid and variable annuities to provide lifetime income benefits without annuitizing. Over two thirds of all annuities opened in America today now have riders, so it is helpful to understand the differences among them.

Consumer Alert: Finding the right annuity agent or advisor for you—an encounter with the Fourth Kind.

Did you know that you can get solid information on annuities without talking to a high pressure salesperson? Advisors who are fiduciaries should be willing to educate you on your choices. Annuities are not well known by all advisors or all fiduciaries however.

For many well-meaning advisors, annuities are a mere sideline. Look for the Certified Annuity Specialist® designation. If someone is showing you only variable or immediate annuities, you need to get a second opinion.

As you become interested in annuities, it is important that you get a firm grounding in the basics, on your own. Getting the right answers implies that you must know the right questions, however. You can find a list of questions to ask any annuity advisor at www.MyAnnuityGuy.com.

You can also view instructional and educational videos on the website without a salesperson hounding you and request free reports.

Research on the internet is a good start, but eventually, you will want to sit down face to face with the **Fourth** kind of agent or advisor— someone who is truly interested in your situation, your goals, and your special concerns and understands the mechanics of portfolio allocation. There should be no sales pressure of any kind.

CHAPTER 13

ANNUITY INCOME RIDERS – THE GOOD, THE BAD AND THE CONFUSING

AN ANNUITY IS A FLEXIBLE FINANCIAL PRODUCT that allows you to accumulate retirement savings within an IRA or on a tax-deferred basis outside of an IRA. You can reap the benefits of your savings in the form of a lump sum payment back to you in five, seven, or 10 years. You can make partial withdrawals along the way or take monthly income. You can even choose a "paycheck for life" with annuitization. Sounds great right? The downside to annuitization is that you can't opt out once you've opted in – you lose all access to your principal.

Enter the Riders.

Certain types of income riders can now be added to hybrid and variable annuities, providing a convenient alternative: lifetime income benefits without the principal lockdown. Over 2/3rds of all annuities opened in America today have riders, so get ready to saddle up. Here's what you need to know.

A Little History

In 2003, income riders became available on variable annuities only to provide a guarantee of income benefits if the markets performed poorly – which they did.

Then hybrid index annuities began adding income and death benefit riders in 2006, and today, virtually all hybrid index annuities offer optional riders, known as Guaranteed Lifetime Withdrawal Benefits (GLWBs).

Riders 101

Annuity riders give you the right, but not the obligation to take a lifetime income in a specific amount, at a specific time, in measured quantities, on a reliable basis, for as long as you want. Essentially, an income rider gives you all the benefits of annuitizing, with slightly less income, without demanding you make an irrevocable commitment. However, you do have to pay a nominal charge for the right to maintain flexibility. When income planners talk about "pensionizing" your income, very often what we're talking about is adding on a rider that allows you to take income that is guaranteed for life, with the right to back out. It's flexible, safe, and low cost, too. Of course, you also have the option of forgoing riders entirely.

But think about this for a moment: The world is a risky place. You're going to live a long time, and you need to know that you have the money to do it. The best way I know to achieve this is through creating pensionized income.

Remember: You will always have money as long as you have income. But you will not have income if you run out of money.

Riders come in two categories: Guaranteed Lifetime Withdrawal Benefits (GLWB) and Guaranteed Minimum Income Benefits (GMIB).

The Need-to-Knows on GMIB and GLWB Annuity Riders

- The goal of GLWBs and GMIBs is the same: Adding another way to ensure a lifetime income for the annuity owner, while maintaining flexibility.
- The GLWB is an optional "add-on" and does not require annuitization. What it does is allow you to "pensionize" your income (maintain control of the principal) without having to annuitize your annuity (lose control). The rider can be dropped at any time, but can't be added later.
- The GMIB is embedded into a variable annuity and leads to annuitization – it's not an add-on feature, but rather a built-in. Often the owner pays fees on the growing rider base, rather than accumulated value. Variable annuities have been

forced to reduce income payouts on their riders due to market realities. Unlike hybrids, which don't depend on market outcomes for revenue, variable annuity revenue can decline for the insurer when markets decline.

	GMIB with Variable Annuity	GLWB with Hybrid Annuity (some variable annuities have GLWBs)
What do the Letters Stand For?	**GMIB =** Guaranteed Minimum Income Benefit	**GLWB =** Guaranteed Lifetime Withdrawal Benefit
Is annuitizing generally required?	Yes	No
How many years do I have to wait for the rider to "kick in" and lock in a lifetime income?	10 years GMIB	0 or 1 year GLWB
Cost of rider	.5 to 1.25%	0 to .95%
What is the typical lifetime payout rate at age **65**?	4% to 5% Must annuitize	5% to 5.5% No annuitization
What are typical payout rates at age **70**?	4% to 5%	6%
What are typical payout rates at age **75**?	4% to 5%	6.5%

These figures were valid as of February 1, 2013. Policies vary greatly, and joint annuitant payouts are generally lower. Contact a licensed annuity professional for an update to current rates and terms. For additional input, visit www.MyAnnuityGuy.com

Shift Happens

The top hybrid fixed index annuity riders now pay more than the top variable annuity riders, with fewer fees. A historical first.

Within those categories are three different kinds of riders: Income Riders, Death Benefit Riders and Long Term Care Riders.

Income Riders: The most popular of these is the Income Rider. By adding an income rider to a variable or hybrid annuity, you give yourself extra ways to fund and plan your retirement.

Death Benefit Riders: These riders protect against declines in principal values due to market conditions for beneficiaries. I.e. If you put $200,000 into an annuity, but market conditions have decreased it's value to $180,000, if you die before taking your money out of the annuity, your heirs will receive the full $200,000.

Long Term Care Riders: If poor health requires you to stay in a nursing home or receive at-home care, this rider will increase your income to help you pay for health care. Long-term care insurance can also be bought individually.

Don't let the term "rider" throw you. It's simply an optional insurance enhancement to an annuity that provides extra benefits of income insurance, like adding on a few deluxe details when buying a new car. You can do without them to keep the cost low, or buy the extra features you need. Most riders cost about 1% per year. This fee is not superfluous. It is used to fund the guarantees for all annuity owners in the pool—like paying into a pension plan at work.

Comparig Income Riders Head to Head—What You Need To Know

DISCLAIMER: *The hypothetical numbers presented here are intended to help you understand the mathematical formulas used by insurance companies to calculate guaranteed income benefits. No particular insurance companies are being represented and no particular annuity product is being recommended (or not recommended.) No financial product is right for everyone. It always pays to compare.*

See your annuity brochure and contract for details. This is a general overview of math concepts to make you a more informed consumer.

Head to Head Comparison #1

Annuity Rider A vs Annuity Rider B

What you want to pay attention to: Note the Income Base Growth Rate on any rider you are comparing. Your eventual income is based on the amount of the Income Base. It grows every year like Social Security. The income = withdrawal rate X Income Base.

Age: 65   Amount: $100,000

HEAD TO HEAD COMPARISON: ANNUITY 'A' VERSUS ANNUITY 'B'								
		ANNUITY 'A'				ANNUITY 'B'		
Year	Age	Income Base Growth Rate	INCOME BASE	WITH DRAW RATE	LIFE INCOME	Income Base Growth Rate	INCOME BASE	WITH DRAW RATE	LIFE INCOME
0	62	4.00%	$200,000	4%	$8,000	6.00%	$200,000	4.50%	$9,000
1	63	4.00%	$208,000	4%	$8,320	6.00%	$212,000	4.60%	$9,752
2	64	4.00%	$216,320	4%	$8,653	6.00%	$224,720	4.70%	$10,562
3	65	4.00%	$224,973	4%	$8,999	6.00%	$238,203	4.80%	$11,434
4	66	4.00%	$233,972	4%	$9,359	6.00%	$252,495	4.90%	$12,372
5	67	4.00%	$243,331	4%	$9,733	6.00%	$267,645	5.00%	$13,382
6	68	4.00%	$253,064	4%	$10,123	6.00%	$283,704	5.10%	$14,469
7	69	4.00%	$263,186	4%	$10,527	6.00%	$300,726	5.20%	$15,638
8	70	4.00%	$273,714	5%	$13,686	6.00%	$318,770	5.30%	$16,895
9	71	4.00%	$284,662	5%	$14,233	6.00%	$337,896	5.40%	$18,246
10	72	4.00%	$296,049	5%	$14,802	6.00%	$358,170	5.50%	$19,699
11	73	4.00%	$307,891	5%	$15,395	6.00%	$379,660	5.60%	$21,261
12	74	4.00%	$320,206	5%	$16,010	6.00%	$402,439	5.70%	$22,939
13	75	4.00%	$333,015	5%	$16,651	6.00%	$426,586	5.80%	$24,742
14	76	4.00%	$346,335	5%	$17,317	6.00%	$452,181	5.90%	$26,679
15	77	4.00%	$360,189	5%	$18,009	6.00%	$479,312	6.00%	$28,759

Income riders vary by annuity and company. Always compare with a fiduciary. The growth of the income base will vary several factors including the income base growth rate and withdrawal percentage. There is no cash value in the rider. Your cash value is contained in the body of the annuity. The rider is an insurance based guarantee of income. If your principal runs out over time, the insurance company guarantees to keep paying you the income stipulated by your guaranteed income rider.

Result: Annuity B pays more income because the company is offering a higher income base growth rate AND a higher withdrawal rate. Note that in year 5, Annuity B guarantees a $13,382 lifetime income. Annuity A only offers $9,733.

Many people who first explore annuities for the first time are expecting them to be listed in the Wall Street Journal or to be perfectly uniform among carriers. This is not the case. Each company offers different features, benefits, and restrictions. Remember that annuity accumulation values and rider Income Benefit values are completely separate figures. The income from the rider is drawn from the accumulation value. The lifetime income is contractual. For additional free information visit www.MyAnnuityGuy.com.

A BRIEF COMPARISON OF ANNUITY TYPES

	Variable Annuity	Immediate Annuity	Deferred Income Annuity (DIA)	Fixed rate Annuity	Fixed INDEX Annuity (FIA)
Is my principal placed at risk in the stock market or bond market?	YES	NO	NO	NO	NO
Do I retain access to my principal for partial withdrawals?	YES	NO	NO	YES	YES
Is my principal protected from stock market losses at all times?	NO	YES	YES	YES	YES
Do I have continuous fee deductions from my principal for life insurance?	YES	NO	NO	NO	NO
May I add an income rider to this annuity to guarantee a lifetime income?	YES	NO	NO	YES/NO	YES
Do I pay for an investment manager? (as an ongoing annual fee taken from principal)	YES	NO	NO	NO	NO

Overview only--See product brochures and Statements of Understanding on fixed annuities. Variable annuities contain securities and therefore are sold by a securities prospectus. Not a promotion for any specific product or company.

*An income rider is available on some but not all fixed annuities. Income riders are optional and are a form of permanent income insurance (like a pension.) Some models of annuities offer a built in rider, with no fee.

Variable Annuity Problem: Over 10 years, a variable annuity owner could pay $120,000 in fees, and the fees never stop until all principal is depleted.

FACT: Typical variable annuities can cost 4% per year. On a $300,000 annuity, that can total $12,000 annually. One of the most popular variable annuities in the country from a very big name insurance company has a 1.5% annual mortality charge (life insurance), a 1.5% income rider charge, and approximately 1% a year for the subaccount management fees. If you call your carrier or your agent, always ask what you are paying for these fees. Don't forget the subaccount management fee! It is often overlooked, because it is not stated in the front part of the prospectus. But it is a big part of how the sausage is made.

FYI: A variable annuity may appear to be doing alright during climbing _bull markets_. But when markets correct downward, as they always do, you will see that the fees are eating into your principal at an alarming pace.

Straight Talk:

The Trouble with Variable Annuities

Variable annuities on the plus side, can offer exposure to the upside of markets on an uncapped basis, but unfortunately come without a principal floor. They work in upward markets but can be very disappointing in flat or down markets. There are too many moving parts to keep track of for most people and fees can average 3% to 4% annually, including life insurance costs, income rider costs, and mutual fund management.

The Trouble with Fixed Annuities

Fixed annuities are plain vanilla, and pay little more than a bank CD.

Things to look out for with some Next Generation Fixed Index Annuities

As I mentioned in an earlier chapter, annuities differ greatly and I reject over 98% of all them. Some hybrid annuities have caps, but still are fine if they are offering exceptional income or in-home long-term care benefits. Don't be too quick to pre-judge. Other annuities have spreads with uncapped participation rates. This approach can result in better accumulation, but your income may not be as strong. Don't let any of this confuse you! I'm happy to help you sort out the differences. An important caution: Many CFP®--Certified Financial Planning Practitioners—have a grasp of immediate and variable annuities. I have found them to be deficient when it comes to fixed index annuities. I have hired and let go two different CFP® practitioners. Very nice people, woefully underinformed on annuities. Very knowledgeable in other areas. Annuities require specialized knowledge! Most stock market advisors do not have the expertise.

Final Word On Guaranteed Lifetime Income Riders

The term "Guaranteed Lifetime Income Riders" is now used to refer to both GMIBs and GLWBs. I lean to the GLWB because it can give you the right, *but not the obligation*, to take a lifetime income in a specific amount, at a specific time, in measured quantities, on a reliable basis, for as long as you want. Essentially, a GMIB income rider may force you to "ANNUITIZE", meaning you hand over control of your principal to the insurance company. The GLWB does not require annuitizing. You get the benefits of a contractually guaranteed income, but you stay in control of your principal and your heirs are protected without having to pay an insurance fee.

Comparison: GLWB Income Riders vs. Immediate Annuities, male Age 65

(for more complete age related comparisons, visit www.MyAnnuityGuy.com and download the IQ Wealth Annuity Buyers Guide.)

Annuity Payouts (in order of most to least)	Life only immedi-ate annu-ity*	Life only with 3% inflation factor (COLA)**	Life with 20 year period certain	GLWB Income Rider w/ 5 year deferral	GLWB Income rider w/ 10 year deferral
Top tier	$550	$392	$486	$687	$1,013[1]
Top tier	$535	$390	$485	$678[1]	$984
Middle tier	$521	$374	$478	$591	$829
Middle tier	$520	$372	$476	$586	$813
Bottom tier	$517	$350	$449	$514	$651
Bottom tier	$516	$341	$435	$512	$649
Average	$526	$369	$468	$594	$823
Annual Avg	$6,312	$4,438	$5,616	$7,136	$9,878

*Note: All updates are time sensitive and accurate at time of writing

**Annuities with Cost of Living Adjusters start out significantly lower than straight level payouts.

[1] Includes in-home long term care benefit. (TYPICALLY, doubles income 5 years, then reverts to original payout) The combination of GLWB income rider adds the advantage of the owner remaining in control of principal. Most annuity buyers do not enjoy annuitizing. (giving control of principal to insurance company.) The GLWB avoids annuitizing.

CHAPTER 14

TRAPS, FEES AND GETTING SMART ABOUT ANNUITIES

10,000 Baby Boomers reach retirement age every day, meaning millions every few years. Their investment habits will likely change as they age. With over seventy million baby boomers entering the time of their lives when they will become more conservative and less concerned about conspicuous consumption, smart investors will make adjustments to their own portfolios—especially if they themselves are Baby Boomers.

Over fifty million people living now are expected to live well into their 80s and 90s. That's 20 to 30 to 40 years of retirement they have to plan for. Consider a male retiree of 60 with a wife of 55. She has strong odds of living to 95. So, Boomers should be planning for 30 to 40 very expensive years. Some will spend those years financially secure, not worried about whether their funds will hold out. But others will not. They will worry.

Social Security may or may not exist decades down the line, and at the very least it will be straining to remain solvent. Few retirees have traditional pensions, and for those who do, many company pension plans are dependent on strained municipal governments and/or the Pension Benefit Guaranty Corp., a government agency and payer of last resort when pension funds go under. It's underfunded by tens of billions.

So, the big question: are you going to be "re-active" or "pro-active" to inevitable trends coming your way? Are you going to spend 20 to 40 years worrying about money? Or are you going to get after it, and create your own pension?

As pensions and defined benefit plans go the way of dinosaurs, many investors are discovering or re-discovering the timely benefits of an often misunderstood class of financial tools known as annuities—which have been improved greatly. Annuities come in many flavors and types which is why there is some confusion over them. Zeroing in the right type of annuity helps to clear confusion and allow for intelligent investigation.

Annuities are rising in popularity with many prominent planners and smart retiring engineers, teachers, and business owners, while the journalist crowd attempts to catch up. Most journalists are as confused as the consumers they write for. One notable exception came recently with journalists Anne Tergesen and Leslie Scism's *Wall Street Journal* article, published June 1, 2012, titled "Getting Smart About Annuities." They warned correctly that some annuities "can be loaded with traps and fees," which is true predominantly with the variable annuity category. Variable annuities have some positives, but they are too expensive and complicated and have hurt the image of annuities in the main stream. Next Generation Fixed Index annuities have gotten rid of the fees and the risk, added exceptional income features and people are noticing.

Tergesen and Scism noted that annuities in general, without help from a knowledgeable fiduciary can be confusing, "But there are valuable ways to use them to build a pension -- and salvage your nest egg." These few sentences correctly sum up the value proposition of annuities in today's environment. Building a pension and salvaging your nest egg are two immensely important things you can do for your portfolio to start enjoying life more and stressing about money less. The journalist's warnings about the fees and risk of variable annuities need to be taken seriously, however. In fact, since the article was written, many new annuities are available.

As their Wall Street Journal article said: "For years, many retirees were content to act as their own pension managers, a complex task that involves making a nest egg last a lifetime. Now, reeling from the stock-market meltdown (of 2008), many are calling it quits -- and buying annuities to do the job for them."

The famed philosopher Kenny Rogers once said, "you gotta know when to hold 'em and know when to fold 'em." There comes a day when you realize you can't keep doing the same things with your money and keep expecting a different and more positive result.

The insanity of keeping too much of your money at risk, invested in assets that don't generate reliable income, must become apparent to you if you are truly going to survive and thrive in the decades ahead.

Did you know? Annuity Holders are Happier People

In a 2004 study, Stan Panis, a director for the Advanced Analytical Consulting Group of Wayland Mass, found that beneficiaries of lifelong-guaranteed income—such as from a privately-purchased annuity or a defined benefit pension, but not from Social Security—were more satisfied in retirement and suffered from fewer depression symptoms than those without such income.

As the report stated "These findings were robust to a multitude of refinements, including joint controls for health status, household income, and marital status. Moreover, the boost in well-being became stronger with duration since retirement date. This finding is consistent with the notion that retirees who rely on finite savings and DC (pension) plan assets grow increasingly worried about funding retirement expenses as they grow older and deplete their assets, whereas recipients of lifelong-guaranteed income, other than from Social Security, are less concerned with outliving their resources."

Panis went on to say: "There is even evidence that retirees with regular paychecks are happier than those who rely exclusively on 401(k)s to supplement their Social Security." The latter "are more prone to depression due to concern about running out of money." Panis is the author of a number of important studies about pensions, annuities and retirement satisfaction.

Tergeson and Scism aptly point out: "The problem: While many investors have a general idea of what an annuity is, few understand the strategies available for making these products a part of their holdings. You have to figure out how much to buy, whether to put your money to work immediately or gradually, and how to invest what remains." I couldn't say that better myself. An annuity is part of the strategy, not the strategy itself. It is coordinated into a plan, and not a product to be compared to a stock or Exchange-traded Fund (ETF). Stocks and ETFs can do things that annuities can't do. Annuities can do things that stocks and ETFs can't do. We don't compare them; we coordinate them into a well-balanced plan.

You shouldn't just go out and buy an annuity, just like you shouldn't buy a stock or ETF in a vacuum. Know what you want your money to do. The purpose of the money dictates its placement, not a high pressure salesperson or a hunch on a stock.

Climbing the Ladder to Make the Most of Annuities

One of the most effective ways to turn less money into more income while maintaining more control over principal is known as *annuity laddering*. Most people have heard of bond ladders. Today, bonds are paying such paltry interest that annuities can readily step up and handle the plan.

The confusion arises, however, when a non-annuity expert tries to apply bond thinking to annuity thinking. It simply won't work. Bond coupon rates and term lengths are registered and are sold as securities. Fixed, immediate and hybrid annuities are not securities – they're different animals than bonds. In fact, in today's low interest rate environment, annuities are superior to bonds on many important levels.

With a bond ladder, you have to time the coupon rate and length of bond to keep the income flowing your way. Many bonds pay quarterly interest, so the planner engages in a somewhat complex layering of bonds that kick in at just the right time. The process is repeated over and over again until a "Rest In Peace" sign is visible from the end of your nose.

Annuity ladders pay more and require far less muss and fuss. If you like to micromanage your investments, and you don't mind extremely low coupon rates, the bond ladder is for you. If you want a more high-tech, low maintenance and durable income plan, consider the annuity ladder.

Bucket Planning with Annuities

Bucket planning, made popular by financial planner Harold Evensky, has been around since the early 1980s, likely originating in bond laddering. It merely refers to planning with a purpose and placing funds into segments, or "buckets," each with its own specific purpose. The choice of what goes in the buckets is critical because the money has to be there at a prescribed time, in the prescribed amount, for the bucket plan to work on a precision basis.

Think of it this way: If you were an astronaut being shot into space, the stages of the rocket spiraling out of Earth's atmosphere are similar to bucket planning. Stage one gets you liftoff, and is based on raw power and thrust. Once its fuel is exhausted, you can see it falling to earth in your rearview mirror. It no longer has value, but it got you to the next stage. Stage two has a precise fuel and power need and a different set of speed requirements. The weight of the first stage is gone; momentum and power are now working against slightly less gravitational pull. You finally break the barrier and head into space, simultaneously dropping stage two, which has served its purpose. You are now enjoying the view and having the time of your life. This is stage is built to take you to your final destination. That part's up to you!

Clearly, you can use all kinds of investments and products to fill buckets, but only annuities are actually built to guarantee that you will make it through all stages, and have the financial fuel to keep going as long as you want.

The Skinny on Fees, Hidden and Otherwise

Smart Money's article "Ten Things Your Variable-Annuity Seller Won't Tell You," quotes an insurance salesman referring to commission as the key reason for selling annuities. Obviously, every financial product comes with a production and delivery cost – and competent, professional assistance also has a value. While *variable annuities* do have continuous fee deductions and are the ones you've probably heard about having "hidden fees," the compensation on *fixed index and hybrid annuities* is actually far less than the long-term costs of many mutual fund portfolios, whose fees never disappear.

It's important to note that compensation for the adviser on fixed index annuities and hybrid annuities does *not* reduce the value of the owner's account. No deduction is made and the client does not pay an advisory fee. One-hundred percent of my clients' assets go to work on day one without reduction by fees.

How to Be Your Own "BS Detector"

There's a battle for your money out there. You need to arm yourself with the facts.

Before you sign on the dotted line of any financial agreement, it's important to have a few facts under your belt about what you're signing and why. These questions are designed to give you a leg up on making smart financial decisions when it comes to your annuities, not to shoot down your adviser. The point is rather to inform yourself so you understand what you're getting into, and make sure your adviser understands what they are getting you into. This is *your* money. Being cautious is smart.

12 Questions You Should Ask *Any* Annuity Adviser (Even Me)

1. Is my principal protected against all market declines?
2. Is the annuity you are trying to sell me a variable, fixed, fixed index, immediate, or hybrid?
3. Can you explain to me in detail, the difference between each kind of annuity, and tell me why you are biased in your recommendation? (Everyone's biased, including me!)
4. How much principal would I have lost in 2002 and 2008 in the annuity you are recommending?
5. How much in total fees would have been deducted from my principal values since 2002 if I owned this annuity?
6. How many years has this company been in business?
7. What are the reserve and capital surplus ratios of this company?
8. How does this annuity grow? I.E. does potential growth come from

   performance of sub-accounts or from interest credited?
9. How long is the surrender charge schedule?
10. What percent of my accumulated values may I withdraw

annually?

11. May I withdraw those funds without penalty in the first year, or must I wait 12 months?

12. 12. Does this annuity come with an income rider?

Had enough? No? Great! I've got 5 bonus questions you should consider asking:

1. If there is an income rider, what is the guaranteed "roll up rate?"

2. If there is an income rider, is there a "floor rate" of growth in the income base, or is it completely market dependent?

3. What is the income rider cost?

4. Exactly what would be my income in year one, year five, year seven, and year 10—in the event of the worst possible market conditions? (If the adviser asks why you are worried about that and starts talking about future market rates of return of 8 percent to 11 percent, ask him or her to put a guarantee on those rates of return) You want to know the worst case. The best case is easy. You don't need an annuity for the best case.

5. What are the total fees deducted every year for Mortality Expense, Administration, and other costs?

Remember to ask these curiously and genuinely, not aggressively or defensively. You are trying to cut through any potential haze and find the right income solution for you in retirement. It's more than okay to be empowered with information: In fact, I recommend it.

The Do's and Don'ts of Internet Research on Annuities

The Internet is a seemingly endless landscape of financial information. But how do you know what information is worth noting, and what information should be left for the vultures? There are hundreds of websites all claiming to be at the top of the financial info game. Some of these sites even have videos with people portraying the illustrious Fortune 500 image. In the end, dazzle and flash be darned, what is most important is you feeling comfortable and getting the answers *you* need and that *you* deserve.

When the time comes for you to get advice on retirement, you do not want to deal with ten people wearing headsets all pushing their way through you and onto the next customer. You want a caring, knowledgeable, and professional licensee—one registered with the state. With no pressure and no rush, you want your questions answered.

So where do you go? Admittedly, I'm biased. I'd suggest my website, MyAnnuityGuy.com, as the best place to start. However, self-promotion aside, what I really want to do is give you the power to make your own choice on what information you take from the Internet and how you make the best financial decisions.

Two Features To Look For in Online Information

1. Diversify, Diversify, Diversify

Those three simple words are not only what makes for a good investment portfolio—they are also the key to great information online. Branch out from blanket statements and people that seem to know all the answers without taking the time to explain their reasoning. Rather, look for websites that offer ways to educate yourself: instructional videos, simple calculators, and critically discussed information.

2. You

Many websites try to take *you* out of the equation when they give advice. In other words, they give generalized statements to all their customers, and then follow up with intense, sales-driven rhetoric. Instead of giving advice, they're making a pitch. And worse, they're not thinking about *you* at all.

Financial information that is focused on *you* has your best financial interests at heart. You'll know it's quality information if it keeps these three points in mind:

1)   Safety: It is vital you make financial investments and decisions that are safe. This is the only way to protect yourself and your family.

2)   Security: Make sure your financial choices are secure and that they make it hard to lose your initial investment. Good financial advice is concerned about your ability to maintain what you have.

3)   Income: All good retirement plans involve an income paid out to you. If the plan doesn't incorporate this, how will you live? Make sure your retirement advice has an income included.

Prepare to Compare

Never settle for the first investment or annuity you see without comparing features, costs, and benefits. Bank advisers or your local insurance agent may be friendly and mean well, but do they allow you to compare more than forty to one hundred annuities? Will they allow you to compare the enhanced income benefits being offered by the top competitive insurers in the marketplace? A good website or financial professional can make that happen for you.

Annuities Online

So now that you know the basics of finding good financial information, let's take a deeper look at how to find stellar info on annuities.

If you take nothing else away from this section, please remember this: First and foremost, make sure you're getting a fair comparison and the best combination of benefits for your dollar before you make any kind of a commitment. So here we go.

The bottom line and best Consumer Advocate's advice on annuities:

1. **Always Compare First and Work with a True Specialist in Hybrid Index Annuities.** Hybrids offer a combination of income, growth, liquidity, and safety with the flexibility to respond to changes in your plan.

2. **Be Clear on How Annuities Work Before You Sign on the Dotted Line.**

3. **Learn How to Retire on 5 percent to 7 percent Safe Withdrawals**.

4. **Educate Yourself on Payouts:** Some annuities may pay you an increasing amount of income every year—learn which ones do AND which ones to avoid.

Two Cautions on Buying Annuities:

1. Don't be confused by marketing techniques offering a 6.5 percent "rate" of interest. The agent is referring to a roll-up rate on an income rider and not to the rate on the annuity itself. Make sure you know how to read the fine print and between the lines.

2. Beware of income riders that require annuitization (handing your principal over to the insurance company). If you are comfortable with annuitizing, fine. But know that there are annuities which do NOT require annuitization that pay excellent income.

General Overview and Summary

This book is not a detailed brochure for annuities, but more of a broad overview. My goal is to help you break through the nonsense you hear about annuities in the popular press and from brokers who hope you don't leave them, so that if one is right for you, you can at least be given the information straight. Now is the time to explore, while you still have your nest egg intact and can plan for an exceptional and satisfying retirement income. Always read your brochures, disclosures, and agreements, like you would with any investment, prior to signing on the dotted line. In closing the chapter on annuities, I'd like to leave you with a few last thoughts:

My 15 Favorite Reasons to Consider Next Generation Hybrid Index Annuities

1. Provides the answer to the question: "Where do I find a way to take my hard earned retirement savings and turn it into a lifelong sustainable income, without making an immediate irreversible decision?

2. Can be the answer to this question: "Where is a safe place for my IRA/401k rollover, that will actually provide a floor under my money, with liquidity and income options?

3. Can be the answer for preserving principal, with the opportunity for conservative to moderate growth from interest rate crediting

4. Can offer upside indexed interest potential with no market downside.

5. Can be a bridge to a future date when annuitization may provide a better opportunity. A great way to "keep your powder dry."

6. Can build an ever increasing future income that does not require annuitizing. Annuitization = loss of control.

7. Can provide security for two lives (you and a spouse or partner.)

8. Replaces uncertainty with a form of absolute return strategy.

9. No annual management or advisory fees..

10. 4 percent to 7 percent guaranteed income account growth with as much as 5 percent to 7 percent safe income withdrawals guaranteed for life, depending on your age. (Annuities vary—for more information and exact quotes, to www.MyAnnuityGuy.com and request more details for annuities approved in your state.)

11. Stepped Up Income as you grow older (on some models) to battle inflation.

12. Access to your money. Most models offer 10% penalty free withdrawals annually (see your documents for details)

13. No upfront fees—100% of your money goes to work on day one with no deductions

14. Sales charges do not reduce your accumulated value

15. More money for your heirs, if that is your goal. Some annuities offer enhanced death benefit riders which can grow your death benefit annually, with no health exam. There are some minimum health standards. See your documents.

Consumer Note:

Annuities today are regulated to protect consumers. Expect a Suitability Report to be part of your application. This report, completed with your agent present, is designed to help the insurance make sure that your portfolio is suited for the annuity. No annuity company that I am aware of will allow you to buy an annuity with most of your portfolio. Although many international and U.S. researchers recommend 70% to 80% of a portfolio be "annuitized", I don't believe there is any insurance company in America today who would accept that allocation. A good planner will help you find the smallest annuity that will solve your needs, not the biggest. The real value of an annuity over traditional investments is that you are rewarded for getting older. This is known as the "mortality credit"— in other words, the older you are the more you can be paid.

Remember, the annuity portion of your financial plan for retirement is just one bucket—the fixed income and preservation bucket. When I put a plan together, we have a Cash Bucket, A Fixed Income Bucket, A Growth Bucket (I prefer funding with quality dividend stocks) and an Insured Outcomes Bucket (to address long term care and any estate planning on your mind.)

Can you accumulate money over time with a Next Generation Hybrid annuity? Yes, but that would definitely require a sit-down with a pro financial planner who is also a fiduciary.

Annuities differ in their main focus. Some annuities are very strong on income and only average on accumulation. Others are strong on accumulation with sub-par income. Why? Because the insurance company only has 100 pennies in a dollar, just like you. It costs them money to provide every competitive benefit. They give up a little "here" to give you more "over there." Most companies offer five to fifteen different annuities (yep, sorry about that!). That's why an honest comparison with no sales pitch is so important

CHAPTER 15

WHAT'S LUCK GOT TO DO WITH IT? THE STORY OF DAVE AND ELLEN

ALL OF US WANT TO THINK we are being scientific about our money decisions. None of us wants to believe we are "winging it" and no one likes to believe they are leaving their futures to chance. But luck plays a big role in investing. When money is being left to accumulate in a consistent strategy over the long run, the role of luck is reduced. When money is suddenly need to create significant pay days from the money we invest, luck enters the picture. Especially if we are relying on markets.

For example, many people tend to retire when the "coast looks clear" in the financial world; think 2007 or 1999—and what happened next. It makes sense. When there are no serious storm clouds on the horizon, you might leave home without a raincoat or umbrella. When markets are rising, unemployment figures look solid, and optimism is in the air, you begin to assume that the time for moving on has finally arrived. Your statements are showing signs of stability, account values in the 401(k) are high, and your debts are paid down. Let's retire!

The chart below depicts the portfolio of Dave, a 62 year old retiring engineer. His 401(k) had grown to a little over $1,000,000 by the end of 1999. His home was free and clear. He and his wife Ellen also owned a cute cabin in the woods, about two hours' drive from their front door. They had around $200,000 in money markets and bank accounts and a stray Roth IRA of around $23,000 for Dave, and $6,000 for Ellen. They had reached their "Number" in their minds: they were millionaires but they never really spoke the word.

Dave caught the wave of the 1980s and 1990s like so many of his buddies at work. A stroke of skill, or a stroke of luck? The markets were on fire in the 90s—so perhaps, luck played a part. No matter, he and his broker had developed a strong relationship, bolstered by the ever rising statement values at the end of the years. Dave had actually outperformed the S&P by a full one percent. Although he paid the advisor 1.5 percent, and the trading costs plus expenses came to another .5 percent, Dave felt that having an experienced advisor was well worth it. With the markets cooperating, life was good.

Then Dave started getting serious about retiring in 1997. He watched the market daily (even hourly sometimes). Once he passed the million dollar mark on his statements, and paid off his mortgages, he and Ellen agreed it was time to see the world. Their net worth was around $1.6 million. He decided to retire in December of 1999.

In early January of 2000, in a ceremonious summit meeting complete with handshakes and hugs, Dave, Ellen and their broker sat down to plan their journey to lasting wealth and to review their 1999 year-end statements, which roughly mirrored the S&P itself. They had been investing in what may go down in history as one of the best 12 year stretches of all time.

They trailed the S & P only slightly after fees. While they attributed the results they got to the "skill" of the advisor, in reality holding an S & P Index Fund would have yielded the same results.

They had averaged an astounding 18.5% over 12 years. When they were ready to pull the plug and retire in 1999, the market was up another 22% for the year. This felt like a clear sign that someone "upstairs" was watching over them. (Although the Bible might have a different take on it.) Their situation seemed ideal. Even if they only averaged 8% on their stocks for the rest of their retirement, they figured they could easily withdraw 5% for life. The idea of doing any special income planning was not even considered. Ellen was 59, and wanted to make sure they could withdraw a level, steady amount of money to sustain their retirement for at least 35 years without coming close to depleting assets. Her mother was still alive at 96 and Ellen anticipated a similar life expectancy. Therefore, without really considering all that could go wrong, they were actually planning to live directly from their savings for 40 years. Would their money last?

True, their Social Security income would be a big part of their plan, but they would drain down cash until both Social Security checks kicked in, and still would need $50,000 annually pre-tax to live the life they dreamed. Together, with their advisor, the three of them decided on a very conservative course of action. Rather than just winging it, they reviewed all expenses once again and calculated inflation going forward. Ellen said she preferred going with the lower amount of income at 5 percent because security was far more important than surplus income. Since the house was recently paid off, and the two of them did not live an overly lavish lifestyle, they concluded that all they would need was $50,000 annually. Rather than withdrawing a higher amount, which they had originally envisioned, they settled on the more conservative and sensible route of withdrawing only 5 percent annually. The three of them all were supremely certain that their portfolio would grow at 7 percent (worst case) and up to 12 percent best case. Subconsciously, they all expected a 9 percent to 10 percent return from their investments. The computer simulator showed them not only receiving the income of $50,000 annually through age 95, but seeing their account grow to more than $2 million. They were set.

The chart below is an approximation of what occurred for Ellen and Dave in real time. As you can see, they ran into the reality known as Sequence of Returns risk. Their average rate of return was over 8%, but they got big losses right out of the chute. This is the problem with online calculators. They show your returns into the future in a straight-line average. But in the real world—especially if you are a stock market investor—returns are random and chaotic, up and down. Yes, Dave and Ellen could start living on less, but that wasn't their dream. With the help of their advisor, who was an accumulation specialist, they had a faulty plan for retirement income, but were unaware. Let's look:

Year	Account Value	Market Result	GAIN/ LOSS IN $$$	ACCOUNT VALUE	LESS Management Fees @ 1.5%	Annual fees in dollars	Income Withdrawn @ 5.0%	TOTAL INCOME RECEIVED	ACCOUNT VALUE
1	$1,000,000	0%	0%	$1,000,000	$985,000	$15,000	$50,000	$50,000	$935,000
2	$935,000	-37%	-$345,950	$589,050	$580,214	$8,836	$50,000	$100,000	$530,214
3	$530,214	5%	$26,511	$556,725	$548,374	$8,351	$50,000	$150,000	$498,374
4	$498,374	16%	$79,740	$578,114	$569,442	$8,672	$50,000	$200,000	$519,442
5	$519,442	5%	$25,972	$545,414	$537,233	$8,181	$50,000	$250,000	$487,233
6	$487,233	11%	$53,596	$540,829	$532,716	$8,112	$50,000	$300,000	$482,716
7	$482,716	29%	$139,988	$622,704	$613,364	$9,341	$50,000	$350,000	$563,364
8	$563,364	-22%	-$123,940	$439,424	$432,832	$6,591	$50,000	$400,000	$382,832
9	$382,832	-12%	-$45,940	$336,892	$331,839	$5,053	$50,000	$450,000	$281,839
10	$281,839	-9%	-$25,366	$256,473	$252,626	$3,847	$50,000	$500,000	$202,626
11	$202,626	21%	$42,552	$245,178	$241,500	$3,678	$50,000	$550,000	$191,500
12	$191,500	29%	$55,535	$247,035	$243,330	$3,706	$50,000	$600,000	$193,330
13	$193,330	33%	$63,799	$257,129	$253,272	$3,857	$50,000	$650,000	$203,272
14	$203,272	23%	$46,752	$250,024	$246,274	$3,750	$50,000	$700,000	$196,274
15	$196,274	38%	$74,584	$270,858	$266,795	$4,063	$50,000	$750,000	$216,795
16	$216,795	1%	$2,168	$218,963	$215,678	$3,284	$50,000	$800,000	$165,678
17	$165,678	8%	$13,254	$178,933	$176,249	$2,684	$50,000	$850,000	$126,249
18	$126,249	30%	$37,875	$164,123	$161,661	$2,462	$50,000	$900,000	$111,661
19	$111,661	-3%	-$3,350	$108,312	$106,687	$1,625	$50,000	$950,000	$56,687
20	$56,687	31%	$17,573	$74,260	$73,146	$1,114	$50,000	$1,000,000	$23,146
21	$23,146	2%	$463	$23,609	$23,255	$354	$50,000	$1,050,000	-$26,745

The above chart is for illustration only. All figures are approximate and hypothetical. Past performance does not guarantee future results.

As you can see, their retirement nest egg was cut in half in 36 months by the exact same force that grew their money: the stock market. What can we learn from Dave and Ellen's situation? There are several points, but these are the important lessons:

1. When planning income withdrawals, you can **never assume** a rate of return for the markets without having a plan for the worst-case scenario.
2. A plan that works in the worst case will shine if the best case happens.
3. Hope is not a strategy.
4. Taking level withdrawals from a fluctuating account can cause early depletion of a portfolio.
5. The Sequence of the returns matters. Had Dave and Ellen experienced continued 20 percent gains for the first several years of their retirement, they would have fared much better.
6. Average return works well as a benchmark in an accumulation portfolio. It can be meaningless in a withdrawal portfolio.
7. Stuff happens.
8. Luck matters.
9. The year you retire can be a major determinant of your future—something over which you have no control, unless you choose guaranteed income assets.
10. A properly structured annuity portfolio can shield an income portfolio against market losses, and guarantee a level and sustainable income for two lives--$50,000 in this case.

Everyone's situation is different, but each of us can learn from "Ellen and Dave." Because of the uncertainty in annual market outcomes, combined with the non-negotiable amount of income you and your spouse will require for a very long time, with no outside income coming in, doesn't it make sense to ensure at least the income portion of your retirement plan?

Retire Smarter: Protect Your Retirement With The Rule of 100

If you get nothing else from this book, get this: You need to be very mindful of the percentage of assets at risk as you reach the age of retirement. The Rule of 100 has also been called the "Age In Bonds Rule," but that name is problematic because bonds are not paying enough to fund retirement, while bond ETFs and mutual funds are actually at their highest risk points for capital losses in more than 35 years.

There have only been two years in history where the value of stocks and value of bonds fell in the same year: 1931, and 1969. At the current time, we could be setting up for number three.

Donald Trump, the ultimate entrepreneur is on record as saying some of his best investments were the ones he didn't make. You don't have to be fully invested in the stock market in retirement. In fact, it may be a very poor idea. That being said, you don't want to turn your back on opportunity. In this massive global market of markets, there is always opportunity. No one denies that, especially me. But in that same massive market of markets, your 401(k), 403b, or IRA can also be seen as an inner tube floating in the ocean. How far from the sight of land should you float? In other words, how much of your precious retirement nest egg should be allocated to risk/opportunity and how much to preservation/income?

Many formulas can work, but one way to starve your problems and feed your opportunities is to use the simple but reliable Rule of 100. Steve Jobs, another titan of business, had this to say:

> **"Simple can be harder than complex: You have to work hard to get your thinking clean to make it simple. But it's worth it in the end because once you get there, you can move mountains."**
>
> Steve Jobs

The Rule of 100 sounds simple but it is based on sound thinking. Simply subtract your age from the number 100. The resulting number is the maximum percent of your investable assets that should be kept at risk, regardless of the opportunity.

Rule of 100

Purpose: Determine the right amount of investment assets at risk

Formula:

100 (–) your age = Maximum percent of investable assets at risk

For Example:

Dave, age 62

Investable assets: $800,000

100 (--) 62 = 38% of investable assets

= $304,000 maximum at risk

=$496,000 in principal protected assets

The Rule of 100 may at first seem too conservative to you. On the other hand, many people will find it too aggressive. No two people are alike. In secular bear markets, I might even add 10 percent to the safe side. In secular bull markets, I might add 10 percent to the aggressive side. This is where an adviser and a retirement coach like myself earns his or her salt.

Discretion is always the better part of valor. It's said on Wall Street that the investor with $10,000,000 is more concerned with a return *OF* principal rather than a return *ON* principal. The investor with less than a million is often chasing after the highest return *ON* principal. This is understandable but it is also a risk. Risk isn't always bad, but a risk must be calculated, have a purpose, have an exit strategy, and have a stop loss built in.

Of the $496,000 in Dave's portfolio, how much should be allocated to an annuity ladder? That's up to Dave, but $200,000 to $400,000 in annuities leaves him and Ellen with plenty of liquidity and the ability to grow $400,000 worth of capital back into $800,000 in a reasonable period of time. How much time? That of course depends on the real-world net rate of return.

The Rule of 72: How Long Will Recovering Lost Money Take?

Using another formula, the Rule of 72, we can see how long it will take for Dave's $400,000 in growth capital to turn back into the original $800,000:

Rule of 72

Purpose: To determine how long it will take to double an amount of money at various rates of return.

Formula: Divide your rate of return into the number 72. The result is the number of years it will take to double.

Example: Dave expects to average a net 7 percent return after fees and expenses, before tax. If he is successful in averaging 7 percent, he will double his $400,000 back into $800,000 in 10.2 years

The Math

72 divided by 7 = 10.2 years to double, turning $400,000 into $800,000

- @9% money doubles in 8 years
- @8% money doubles in 9 years
- @6% money doubles in 12 years
- @4% money doubles in 18 years
- @1% money doubles in 72 years

How the Rule of 72 Works in ACCUMULATION portfolios, Prior To Retirement

When you first see the devastating effects of Reverse Dollar Cost Averaging (Chart 1) it is startling. Realize that both Dave and Ellen eventually will have Social Security coming in. They also had a set income goal in mind from their assets of .

Still, questions arise:

1. How can money disappear that fast?
2. Are the figures really correct?
3. Why did Dave keep taking the same amount of money out?
4. Why did he stay in the pie chart portfolio—shouldn't he have moved to safer places?
5. What if the fees and expenses were higher or lower?
6. What if he didn't average 7 percent in years 11-20?
7. What if Dave and Ellen had an emergency and had to tap into their nest egg in a big way?
8. What if one or both of them end up needing long term care?
9. What if Dave dies?
10. Aren't there a lot of variables?

There are even more questions to ask, which is why planning is not as simple as it first may appear.

Let's review some answers:

1. **How can money disappear that fast?** It only looks fast in retrospect. Every financial problem is easier when you look back 10 years or 25 years later—hindsight is always 20/20. While it was happening, Dave was processing information the way that everyone does: moving from Optimism, to Excitement, to Elation, to Concern, to Nervous, to Alarmed, to Frightened, to Relieved, to Optimistic. Dave experienced all of that and more over a very normal and natural 10 year period. The reality is that Dave continued to read the papers, surf the

internet, and watch the talking heads. Hope was always on the horizon, which is another key lesson: **Wall Street is in the business of selling hope.** Reverse dollar cost averaging is pure math, and pure math is what you need to pay attention to in the WITHDRAWAL phase of your money career—if you ever want to be lounging on that yacht.

2. **Are the figures really correct?** Yes, please check my work.

3. **Why did Dave keep taking the same amount of money out?** Because Dave and Ellen had built their dreams over 30 years of saving and investing. Dreams die very hard and optimism springs eternal. The advisor's strong recommendations were to "stay the course" and be patient. "Selling now only locks in a loss." Remember those platitudes from **Chapter 7**? While these pieces of advice may be solid in the ACCUMULATION phase, they can have disastrous consequences in the DE-CUMULATION phase. Dave and Ellen were applying elements of accumulation strategy to a de-cumulation portfolio

4. **Why did he stay in the pie chart portfolio—shouldn't he have moved to safer places?** See question 3.

5. **What if the fees and expenses were higher or lower?** See both charts in this chapter.

6. **What if he didn't average 7 percent years 11-20?** See chart 2.

7. **What if Dave and Ellen had an emergency and had to tap into the nest egg in a big way**? Yeah, right? Now you're starting to sound like me.

8. **What if one or both of them end up needing long term care?** See my next book. Hint: A long term care rider is a solid solution in most cases.

9. **What if Dave dies?** Ellen could be in serious financial trouble without proper planning.

10. **Aren't there a lot of variables?** Yes, there really, really are. That's why the key factor is separating your emotions from the mathematics. Use math-driven assets to pay yourself an

income. Use market-driven investments to attempt to grow money over the long term. Don't cross your wires. Stay on purpose—the purpose of money should dictate where you put it to work, not optimism about market outcomes. Hope is not a strategy.

We have established that losing money in one or two years of retirement, while simultaneously withdrawing significant capital can create a serious decline in working capital. Let's treat your portfolio as a business and apply business management principles for a moment. Fair enough?

Practical Hindsight

Hindsight is always 20/20. In real time, Dave was processing information the way that everyone does: moving from Optimism, to Excitement, to Elation, to Concern, to Nervous, to Alarmed, to Frightened, to Relieved, to Optimistic. Dave experienced all of that and more over a very normal and natural 10 year period. The reality is that Dave continued to read the papers, surf the internet, and listen to the talking heads. Hope was always on the horizon, which is another key lesson: Wall Street is in the business of selling hope. *You're in the business of retiring with your shirt intact.* Reverse dollar cost averaging is pure math, and is your biggest risk when taking income.

Build Retirement Wealth The SMART Way.

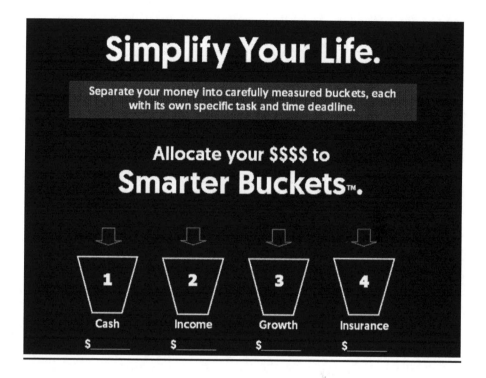

CHAPTER 16

THE IQ WEALTH SMARTER BUCKETING SYSTEM™
--THE STRATEGY THAT WILL GIVE YOU A
LIFETIME OF INCOME AND FINANCIAL
PEACE OF MIND...FROM NOW ON

ALTHOUGH MY FIRM IS SKILLED IN GROWING MONEY, my key expertise lies in creating income in retirement: Income that lasts, that is sustainable and that will not let you down when you need it the most. My goal isn't just to fund your retirement and meet your expenses. My goal, and the work I do, can help you **overfund** your retirement, help you live life on your terms and do what you want, when you want to do it.

In other words, no money worries – no matter what.

My strategy, known as **The IQ Wealth Smarter Bucketing System ™**, will help you prevent lifestyle decline, which plagues many Americans in their late 70s and 80s. What went wrong? Their plans simply did not work. In many cases they didn't have a plan, or they followed the time-worn Rules of Thumb that don't work like they used to. It doesn't have to be that way for you.

Many of these retirees assumed banks would be paying 6 percent on CDs forever. It never dawned on them that:

- **"Shift"** happens.
- **Economies** change.
- **Markets** change.
- Emotional, Physical, Spiritual, and Financial Needs **change.**
- **Adapting to change** is the key to success at any age.

I've found that too much financial advice is thrown around by TV and Radio gurus that simply doesn't apply to all age groups, especially yours. It's getting hard to separate entertainment from information, fact from fiction. That's part of my job as an advisor—to sort out the information that you can put to work to satisfy your purpose in life.

What Is The IQ Wealth Smarter Bucketing System™?

The IQ Wealth Smarter Bucketing System™ is a long-term strategy designed to create contractually guaranteed income from properly selected segments of your portfolio. It uses a combination of cash generating investments, hybrid and immediate annuities, and in some cases, specially funded cash value life insurance to achieve income and legacy goals. The strategy begins with the end goal in mind—meaning that they non-negotiable element of a well thought retirement investment plan should do many things, but not fool around when it comes to replacing the income from your working days.

The IQ Wealth Smarter Bucketing System has these key objectives:

1) **Consistent monthly cash flow.** Our goal is to generate a monthly cash flow in the range of 5 percent to 7 percent on a lifetime basis, without risking principal to market declines. We keep fees at a minimum. We utilize specifically chosen investments and income instruments that combine the right combination of income and lowered risk.

2) **Ample liquidity.** The IQ Wealth Smarter Bucketing System™ measures your specific need for liquidity, both on an everyday basis and for emergencies.

3) **Inflation protected growth.** Your income and your various assets may need to increase on a regular basis to keep up with inflation. The IQ Wealth Smarter Bucketing System™ combines contractual growth, strategic growth, infrastructure investments, and layered compounding to keep the strategy responsive to inflation.

4) **Family protection.** Once again we begin with the end in mind. If leaving your heirs safe and secure is important, The IQ Wealth Smarter Bucketing System™ uses financial building blocks with powerful guarantees that have not failed in 100 years.

5) **Protection of capital from market declines –alleviation of interest rate risk.** Today's stock and bond markets are at risk of a historic "Double Whammy" which has occurred only two times in history: 1931 and 1969. This is a quirk of finance that can only occur when interest rates are at historic lows and the market flirts with all-time highs.

The Six Pillars of The IQ Wealth Smarter Bucketing System™

<u>**How To Restore Balance To Your Financial Plan**</u>

Prudent retirement investing has always been expressed as a pyramid of assets. Common sense has always endured, as has the principle of building structures with the heaviest, strongest materials at the bottom. The Egyptian Pyramids are a monument to solid engineering and common sense. The concept is to build heavy from the bottom and go thinner and lighter as you near the top because the risk increases. It doesn't pay to mess with gravity or high winds.

In your financial plan, the principles are identical. The safest, most secure assets should be laid in at the bottom, like poured concrete over rebar. This is the base of your structure. If you are going to skimp, don't skimp on the foundation. A sound foundation is not merely a cost; it is an investment in long-run endurance and stability.

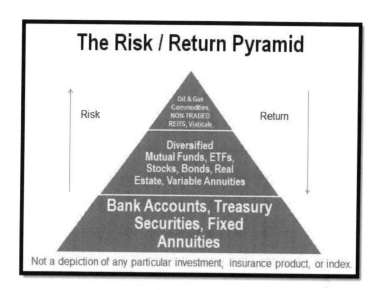

Violating the rules of solid construction and engineering usually ends badly. Maybe not today, maybe not tomorrow, but one day. With the investment pyramid, we want to build upon the foundation of safety and security. Let's build a structure that will look the same 40 or 50 years from now. There's a place for riskier, illiquid investments right up at the top in small quantities. We may repaint, put a new roof on, new siding, new windows, or re-carpet down the road, but let's start with a bottom-heavy, level and plumb foundation, built with sound materials.

All financial planners were taught this most basic of principles, yet many portfolios today show preference and over-allocation to Non Traded REITs, commodities (including ETFs juiced with derivatives), and variable annuities. Many investors are loaded with REITs, target date funds and 60/40 stock fund/bond fund portfolios as their foundations. You can't build a foundation on shifting sands.

In other words, today, many retirees and pre-retirees have turned the pyramid upside down. They are **D**iversifying **U**nder **M**isguided **B**eliefs.

A symptom of the New Normal:

The Reversal of the Investment Pyramid

The Problem

Non-traded REITS and Mutual Funds have moved to the base of many financial plans, while secure, pensionable products are missing. This is an unsustainable trend with little protection against both Sequence of Returns Risk and Longevity Risk. This may plague investors as they mature--unless they get S.M.A.R.T.

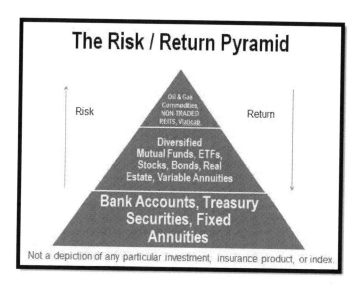

The Solution: Restore Balance and Sleep Well At Night With the IQ Wealth Smarter Bucketing System™

It's Not What You Make, It's What You Keep That Counts, AND What Keeps Coming Your Way. Cash flow, not cash, is the new king. Build permanent passive cash flow into the foundation of your financial plan. More income, smarter investments, and more for those you care about most.

©Copyright 2012/2013 by IQ Wealth Management

The secret to success of the IQ Wealth Smarter Bucketing System™ is that it begins with the end in mind:

Keeping it *simple* isn't stupid:

1) **An income replacement plan.** The shift from the accumulation phase to the de-cumulation phase means you will have to make a living from your investments and products, and it has to last.

2) **A tax reduction plan.** The IRS wants their fair share-- let's not give them a dollar more.

3) **A plan for pensionized income, on demand.** The move from defined benefit pension plans to defined contribution plans gave investors more freedom but left them with more uncertainty. Pensions made life easier. Retirement shouldn't be about stressing over markets. The right annuities can preserve liquidity and create a safe "pension-on-demand."

4) **A plan for risk management.** Business cycles are constantly changing, meaning recessions, corrections, inflations, Black Swans and health care issues never go away. Most investors have played offense their entire lives, but defense wins championships. How good is your defense?

5) **A plan for assisted care.** In case of a health setback or assistance needs with daily living.

6) **The coordination of both the income plan and the estate plan.** Who gets what? How much? And when? How are your assets titled? Have you done a life insurance review lately? This isn't as hard as it looks when you begin with the end in mind.

Why Does The IQ Wealth Smarter Bucketing System™ Focus On Cash Flow?

Most traditional investments are based on the concept of capital appreciation. You buy assets, such as shares of stock, and hope they appreciate in value so you can sell them later for a profit. Cash-flow investing works differently. With cash flow, you buy an asset not for its future value but for its ability to generate income. This income gives you flexibility: You can spend it if you want to or you can reinvest it. Cash flow reinvested is compounding growth. Cash flow that keeps you happily above water at all times: Priceless.

There's no doubt that traditional investments worked in traditional times, but there's nothing traditional about the market cycles of today.

Knowledge is Wealth—Separating Fact From Fiction When Building Your Income Plan

In retirement, the rubber meets the road. A 30-year-old has a much different set of rules, timeframes, and freedoms than the investor aged 60 or 70. An investor of 30 gets their income in the form of a paycheck every week or two, and they get raises over the years to battle inflation. Because of that paycheck, the young investor may be oblivious to the risk, and is justified in approaching Wall Street cavalierly. Youth must be served.

However, an investor of 60 or 70 can't afford to be oblivious. True, markets tend to recover when given time, but when it's your time (and retirement fund) being given away, time becomes your most precious commodity.

Will the advisor who got you to retirement—the one who specialized in the art of accumulation—truly be the advisor to take you through retirement? A good advisor is like a good surgeon. Your general practitioner may be well-rounded in the knowledge and application of every day health care. (In the new normal you will be seeing their assistant more than the doctor, but that's a different story for a different day). When you need surgery, however, you don't want your general practitioner.

The same is true with investing. The avalanche of information and the tens of thousands of different investment choices require hands-on dedication, full time study, and hours of time exploring the pathways to growth.

Investing used to involve finding good companies with great dividends and corporate earnings, priced at under 10 times earnings. You could take your time, read books on investing, go the library, review shareholder's reports, and generally count on the company maintaining leadership within its industry and sector. Today, that kind of approach generates an "LOL," or "OMG" as the kids say. It just doesn't work.

The market now moves at a jaw-dropping, breathtaking pace. Over a trillion dollars a day in securities changes hands. High frequency traders and hedge funds now dominate 75 percent of all trades on the New York Stock Exchange and Euronext markets. Morningstar now reports there are over 100,000 indexes that can be traded, let alone individual investments. Trades are being made by robots overseen by computers managed by Dark Pools in large warehouses in close proximity to the exchanges (for greater computer speed). Your bank account is measured in hundredths of a percent, but the speed at which the ETFs in your 401(k) or IRA are being traded on the open markets (not necessarily by your manager) is being measured in *milliseconds*.

In the time you go to Costco and back, saving $47 on groceries (and buying $44 in clothing you didn't need), a hundred billion dollars' worth of securities changed hands. It's almost a certainty that ETFs and funds that you hold are right in the thick of it all.

Your Note To Self:

Q. Will the advisor who got you *to* retirement truly be the advisor to take you *through* retirement?

A. A good advisor is like a good surgeon. Your general practitioner may be brilliant and well-rounded in the knowledge and application of every day health care. (In the new normal you will be seeing their assistant more than the doctor, but that's a different story for a different day). When you need surgery, however, you don't want your general practitioner.

You want the specialist best equipped at taking care of the need at hand—someone who focus full time energy and research on your issue.

Your issue is **preserving** your capital and **sustaining** your income through thick and thin markets. You want to wake up from a good night's sleep one day, ten years from now, feeling really satisfied about your financial plan...not because you dodged a bullet and got lucky, but because a plan came together. **Decumulation** planning is the polar opposite of Accumulation planning. Seek a retirement coach skilled in the area of decumulation, who can help you with a S.W.A.N. strategy (Sleep Well At Night), as well as your growth investments. A specific, measurable, attainable, reliable, and timely plan can be yours.

CHAPTER 17

SMART IS THE NEW RICH: HOW TO INSURE YOUR INCOME, INSURE YOUR OUTCOMES AND INVEST THE REST WITH PURPOSE®

A FULLY INTEGRATED RETIREMENT PLAN must include an income replacement plan, an investment plan, a tax plan, a healthcare plan, and an estate plan. However, most people don't have a complete plan in any one of those areas let alone all five.

With pensions disappearing and recessions wearing down portfolios over the past 12 years, the primary concern today is: "How do we take our accounts and use them to generate secure, sustainable lifetime income regardless of what the markets do?"

With the help of some of the brightest minds in the retirement planning industry, I've developed proven strategies to reduce or eliminate the anxiety historically related to retirement planning. The objective is to balance a retirement portfolio to build fixed income security that is safe, measurable, attainable, reliable and timely. The income replacement plan must work in harmony with a legacy plan and a plan for growth. Each priority can be assembled into one cohesive whole.

Notice I didn't say "blend." I believe the old fashioned pie chart model mixes and blends too many opposing forces into a problematic pastry with little chance to overcome difficult planning predicaments. Some issues can be addressed with exposure to markets. Others are best solved mathematically, and backed by contractual guarantees. Blending and mixing are fine for the Iron Chef™ but not for you, the retiree who must now live off your money in a style that you've been planning for years. As the late, great

Stephen Covey might say, "Begin with the end in mind."

In the future, it won't be about how much money you have, but how much money you have coming in—and what you are able to do with it.

Cash *flow,* not *cash* is king. Being smart with the placement of your money, based on its proper purpose, is the new rich. Permanent cash flow allows you to satisfy ambitions, instead of just covering obligations. Having steady money coming in allows you to go where you want to go. True, life is a journey, but it takes money to reach your destination.

What Is The IQ Wealth Smarter Bucketing System™?

The IQ Wealth Smarter Bucketing System™ is a long-term strategy designed to generate income without depleting your portfolio. Rather than depending on markets, it depends on math and actuarial science combined with guarantees backed by a system of regulated reserves.

The **IQ Wealth Smarter Bucketing System™** has three main objectives:

1) Consistent monthly cash flow, now or in the future @ 4%-7%. (up to 9% or more, depending on age and deferral period)
2) Ample liquidity.
3) Preservation of capital and legacy motives.

Why Does The Well-Built Retirement Plan Focus On Cash Flow And Preservation?

Most traditional investment plans are based on the concept of capital appreciation and speculative gain. You buy assets, such as shares of stock, and hope they appreciate in value so you can sell them later for a profit. Cash-flow investing works differently. With cash flow, you buy an asset not for its future value to grow in size, but for its ultimate capacity to generate income. This income gives you maximum flexibility and is the lowest cost form of financial independence. Even if you run out of principal but still have a rock star income, you will always feel wealthy. If you are sitting on free-and-clear real estate in the form of vacant land or homes, with no cash flow, you can feel very poor.

A Million Just Doesn't Buy What It Used To...

A million dollars in the bank no longer ensure a lifetime of security. Even without a major market decline, stocks will have a thorny path trying to return 6 percent, let alone 10 percent over the next 10 years. This assertion is based on the higher P/E (price to earnings) ratios of today, combined with low dividend yields. The outlook for stocks is meager at best, according to industry giants like Bill Gross and Mohammed El Erian of Pimco, and John Bogle of Vanguard. Gross foresees a maximum annualized growth rate in stocks of around 4 percent. Bogle calculates it at 2.5 percent. Similar conclusions are reached by mathematical analysts, such as Ed Easterling at Crestmont Research. The Federal Reserve has laid down the gauntlet for savers: Low interest rates for as long and as far as the eye can see.

That's fine if you want a mortgage, but not so fine if you want to live off the interest. A startling 2008 Ernst & Young study concluded that a married couple nearing retirement without a defined benefit retirement plan had more than a 9/10 likelihood of outliving their financial assets if one of them lived to age 95. Most people aren't aware of that the risk is this high. In a 2012 study, Ernst & Young performed 2000 Monte Carlo computer simulations based on traditional portfolios of 60 percent stocks and 40 percent bonds. The study was the first of its kind to explore the effects that today's historically low interest rates may have on a de-accumulating retirement portfolio over the long-term. They found that markets are going to have to perform on the high side of history and investors will be required to be exceptionally disciplined in order to avoid a 54 percent chance of running out of money for those retiring today.

Hi Ho, I Still Owe, So Off to Work I Go

Today, many people are retiring with mortgages and no pension, the opposite of their parents and grandparents who retired with no mortgage and a full pension. With life expectancies increasing, the math is not favorable. Many retirees are staying on the job longer. It's good for them, but it is reducing opportunity for younger workers who are expected to pay into the social security system and contribute to the economy. Some retirees will go back to working a job during retirement and like the idea. Others may be forced to do so because finances are running thin. At some point, they may want the job, but the job may not want them. It is also unlikely to find the kind of work or paychecks hoped for - if 25 and 35-year-olds are having trouble finding work, 65 and s70 year olds won't fare much better.

One day, your investments will be required to do the work that you once did. Your money has to last and it has to generate consistent sustainable income. But what income strategy can be counted on to be there in good markets and bad? You won't find it in a target date fund or an ETF. But you can find it at a legal reserve insurance company.

Be Smarter Than Flipping A Coin

Multiple scientific studies have been done over the years to confirm the probability of coin flipping—as in, which comes up more, heads or tails? Every study ends the same: If you only flip a coin 10 times, the outcome ranges from 10 heads in a row (1 in 1,023 chance) to 10 tails in a row (1 in 1,023), and any combination in between. If you flip a coin 10,000 times, the result will be very close to 50/50, heads and tails. Experimenters have done a million coin flips to confirm this (seriously).

If you think of each year in the stock market as a coin flip, you will gain a healthy perspective on how to simplify your portfolio and make some very smart moves with your money that you will never regret. You don't need scientific experiments to know that the odds of 10 positive years in a row are very slim. Does anyone really know where the market will be a month from today?

The Trend Is Your Friend - Until It Isn't

Traders have said this for years. It happens to be truer than ever once your time horizon is shorter. There was a time in history when investors actually invested in stocks for the *"long term,"* however, with the advent of the internet, online investment access and high speed trading, those days are gone. The rise of E-Trade, and Scottrade, and ETF's and "high frequency trading" has led to a market where the bulk of the daily price action in stocks is driven by the direction of the overall market.

A trillion dollars a day is changing hands. The entire market is either risk on, or risk off. The 1000 point "Flash Crash" in 2012 was a small tremor, and a glimpse into what can happen when one set of algorithms sets off another chain of algorithms. When that happens, throw out every rule of investing you've ever learned.

The Greater Fool Theory, Revisited

In this kind of environment investors are generally better served understanding, and investing, with the trend or direction of the overall market rather than *"hoping"* their investments will work out. Don't ever think you are faster than the market. Most people will not sell at the sign of a 10 percent loss. They will wait until they are down 15 or 20 percent—to confirm the losing trend. Currently, markets may be looking "all clear" because the Fed is pumping money into the system. Underneath it all are economic trends that are troubling. Both imports and exports are falling at the same time again. This action has always preceded a recession. If $85 billion a month from the Fed can't inspire a dramatic liftoff in the economy, what is it going to take? And when will you realize that a cyclical bull market is just that—cyclical. With unemployment and slow growth becoming normal in this new economy, where is the *"escape velocity"* required to ignite healthy growth?

The Bank Way, The Wall Street Way, or The Insurance Way—Which Will Lead To The Most Successful Retirements by 2020, 2030, and 2045?

In 2008 the Congressional Budget office reported that Americans lost over $2 trillion in accumulated retirement assets in their 401(k)s, 403b's and other retirement savings in just 15 months, plus another $4 trillion in home values. For many, 10 years of stock market growth was gone in 10 weeks. Not one person who owned a Fixed Index Annuity lost a penny due to the market declines. The term "putting a floor" under your retirement money—and the reason why that is vitally important-- became clearly defined.

The value of an annuity in your financial plan may not be as apparent when markets are calm or rising, just as the value of seat belts or airbags aren't apparent on a Sunday afternoon drive. We don't consider the cost of the seatbelts or the airbags as a detriment as we check on our kids or grandkids in the rear view mirror. Security has value. It can be purchased for small amounts relative to the ultimate benefits. Annuities don't cost, they pay. They are worry-free. The right annuity, or ladder of annuities in your portfolio can take away much of the risk with which you are currently riding down the road. Your employer may not have offered you a pensionized income, but your annuity can offer you one that can start whenever you command.

The Wall Street Way can never lead to lasting confidence about your investments, unless you force a positive attitude in the face of mounting research to the contrary. Just remember: Dale Carnegie was never as rich as Andrew Carnegie - real money and real strategies trump positive thinking. The Bank Way can't win in this low interest rate environment. As a proud bank account owner, you are lending money to the bank at 1 percent. They are lending it at 4 percent to 18 percent, a markup of 400 percent to 1800 percent.

That home equity line of credit looks like the bank is giving money away. Don't worry about the banks. They'll be okay. Will you, if you keep too much of your money there?

The Insurance Way is the least publicize and most criticized by Wall Street promoters. Of course. What fun would it be if everyone decided to cut their risk and fees and move to income based on regulated reserves and actuarial math?

The IQ Wealth Smarter Bucketing System™--A Strategy For More Reward With Less Risk

Years ago, retirement planning was fairly easy. Many people were covered by a pension plan that guaranteed a set monthly income for life. Those days are long gone. Today, you're likely covered under a defined contribution plan, like an IRA or 401(k), or you have rolled over to a self directed IRA. This shift in retirement savings has exposed you to increasing levels of risk. Traditional "pie chart" planning may not adequately address your income or estate planning needs.

- Market Volatility – The closer you are to retirement, the more you're hurt by a plummeting market. Over the past 12 years, despite violent swings in the market, the S&P 500 has barely produced returns of a percent a year. Many are questioning if the market is still a safe or profitable place to keep retirement savings.

- Longevity – The main reason retirement planning is so difficult? You don't know how long you'll live.

- Inflation – You don't know what a loaf of bread will cost in 20 years. For reference, visit the National Debt Clock

CHAPTER 18

WELCOME TO THE NEW NORMAL, PARTING THOUGHTS

THE FINANCIAL RULES YOU AND I GREW UP on no longer apply. Today the markets are ruled by algorithms, government debts are careening out of control, market swings of a thousand points a day are not uncommon, and politicians hate each other. No one knows where the markets are really headed.

Additionally, as you mature your capacity for risk changes. Are you thinking, *"Here we go again, someone else telling me to dial down the risk because I'm getting old?"* No, that's not my point at all (well, maybe part of my point). The point is good investing takes time. You know all the old rules: "buy and hold," "never buy and hold," "diversify," "buy on the rumor, sell on the news," "the first loss is always the best one," "don't fight the Fed," "know when to cut your losses," and "let your profits run, hedge your risks." They may have worked well for you while you were working, but when you retired, so did those Rules of Thumb.

Your income plan for retirement in the new normal must be S.M.A.R.T. and built around more than just rate of return:

- **S**ustainable - Your income must last as long as you do. Period.

- **M**easurable – In dollars. You can't manage what you can't measure.

- **A**ttainable - Your income needs to be real, not based on hope.

- **R**eliable - Cash flow with no interruption, even in poor markets.

- **Timely** - The income is ready for you when you are ready for it.

Good planning in retirement begins with income planning. Building the income floor is the first order of business, just as pouring a concrete foundation is the first step in building any structure. Therefore, smart assets in retirement generate cash flow safely. They have regulated requirements for safety based on financial reserves and are audited by regulatory authorities.

Smart Is The New Rich: Sustainable Cash *Flow*, Not Just Cash, Is The Essence of Real Planning. To Make Your Money Last, Think Income.

In the Old Normal, you could have afforded a haphazard plan. All you needed was a paid off house, money in the bank, some muni bonds and Ginnie Maes, maybe a life policy, and you were good to go. In the new normal, that same plan will pay you a poverty wage and, perhaps, leave your family with very little.

Today, Wall Street circulates the notion that you "need" a million – or even two million - in order to retire. Hearing that, you keep taking layers of risks in order to achieve the elusive and much ballyhooed "Number." You just might need that much, if you take a few more hits like 2008. Even without another "Black Swan," what if you don't get a good return on your investments? What if your fees neutralize your dividends? What if you fail to do income planning now – while your assets are intact – but instead wait for the market to edge higher, then trip? Regression to the mean is inevitable. The higher she goes, the farther she falls.

Success leaves clues: Paying down debts and securing income are the marks of a well-planned retirement. Stop thinking growth; start thinking income. You will never regret it.

Jeffrey Opdyke writing in the *Wall Street Journal* pointed out that an annuity holder with $600,000 placed in annuities could live as well on as a traditional investor with $1,000,000 in stocks and bonds. That's buying the future at a $400,000 discount. Annuities don't cost, they pay. After 2008, the annuity holder with $600,000 in annuities still had $600,000 in annuities with income guaranteed. The investor with a million in the markets likely was down to around $500,000, with confidence shaken.

As always in financial planning, there is no "one-size-fits-all" solution to every set of circumstances. Annuities aren't right for everybody nor are they ever right in unlimited amounts for anybody. However, when clear thinking about statistical fact and academic research get applied to the finite realities of managing money, annuities can't be ignored.

> **"The consensus of the literature from professional economists is that lifetime income annuities should definitely play a substantial role in the retirement arrangements of most people. How great a role depends on a number of factors, but it is fair to say that for most people, lifetime income annuities should comprise from 40% to 80% of their retirement assets under current pricing. Generally speaking, if a person has no bequest motive, or is averse to high risk, the portion of wealth allocated to annuities should be at the higher end of this range."** – Professor David Babbel of the Wharton School of Business, University of Pennsylvania

As startling as it may sound to most investors, there are tens of thousands of annuity owners in America who really couldn't care less what the stock market does this year. Their homes and debts are paid off, their annuities are safe, and their money will roll in come heck or high water. If the market rises, Hybrid annuity owners can enjoy a proportionate rise in value according to a mathematical formula. If the market falls, they won't lose a penny because there is a floor under their money. Their current and future incomes will remain intact.

Critics will say, what about the caps? They'll say, "What about the floor?" This isn't 1995. It's 2013. You've tucked away some money. You don't need the fleeting promise of an unlimited upside; you need protection from the unlimited downside. You need a floor under your retirement money. You need an annuity.

While magazine journalists often display a lack of research, others like Professor David Babbel of the Wharton School of Business report findings as follows:

> **"Lifetime income annuities may not be the perfect financial instrument for retirement, but when compared under the rigorous analytical apparatus of economic science to other available choices for retirement income, where risks and returns are carefully balanced, they dominate anything else for most situations.**
>
> **When supplemented with fixed income investments and equities, it is the best way we have now to provide for retirement. There is no other way to do this without spending much more money, or incurring a whole lot more risk coupled with some very good luck."**
>
> – Dr. Babbel, Wharton School of Business

Wharton is merely one of many academic institutions that have documented the intelligence of using annuities to anchor a retirement portfolio. They don't endorse any annuities. They merely have conducted pure research. Others include: MIT, Berkeley, Chicago, Yale, Harvard, London Business School, The University of Illinois, Hebrew University, and Carnegie Mellon. The researchers included PhDs, actuaries, Nobel Prize winners, and Masters in Accountancy. The evidence is conclusive: Annuities need to be a part of a retired person's financial plan in 2013 and beyond.

What We Mean by "Smart is the New Rich"

In the past, "rich" meant having the biggest pile of cash, the least debt, and the most lucrative pension upon retirement. Worries about markets and economies became a thing of the past on retirement day, if they ever really were a concern in the first place. Life was more orderly then. CNN, FOX, and CNBC were not even a glint in the eye of the networks, and today's retirees still wore letters on their sweaters. Bank accounts earned plenty, bonds did a little better, and the pension handled the rest. It was Miller Time. Rich was easy to define.

How is rich defined today? Is it the person with the biggest house in the best neighborhood, with the finest clothes, the most German or Italian cars, the big name stock broker, and the biggest 401(k)? Or is it the person with the least debt, paid off cars, and a couple of annuities paying like clockwork? Who is smarter? Whose portfolio is truly built to last and whose future looks more certain? It can't hurt to have a large 401(k) or 403b, but keeping it large will be a challenge.

Today, bank rates are near zero and pose a double threat to the retiree. If you buy bonds and CDs held to maturity, your portfolio's overall yield is reduced to dangerous levels. If you invest in bonds via shares of mutual funds or ETFs, your share values stand to decline when interest rates on bonds rise again.

The properly chosen annuity can be the missing puzzle piece in your financial plan. At the very least, make sure your mind is open and you take the time to explore. As the world gets more turbulent and financial markets more unpredictable, you will one day thank yourself for having extra AFORI (Alternative Forms Of Retirement Income.)

"Being rich is having money. Being wealthy

is having time."

-Stephen Swid

IQ WEALTH PLAN	Investing FOR Retirement, age 20 to 59	Investing DURING Retirement, age 60+	Taking Income In Retirement, age 60+
Investment Objectives	Accumulation, Contribution	Preserve Principal	Withdraw at a safe sustainable rate
Return on Investment	Seek higher diversified yields	Seek realistic, moderate yields	Seek cash flow that won't run out
Risk	Adjust risk to time horizons, use dollar cost averaging	Broadly diversified among asset classes, moderate	Seek contractually guaranteed lifetime income with annuities—avoid reverse dollar cost averaging
Taxes	Seek tax deferral. Explore Roth IRA if practical	Explore tax reduction strategies, ROTH conversion, POSSIBLY oil and gas MLPs	Roth IRA withdrawals, and if tax qualified, cash value life insurance policy loans
Annuities	Not suggested prior to age 40, annuities with GLWB rider after 40—ok for partial allocation	Yes, explore the proper use of annuities. Seek lowest fees, highest income.	Yes, explore annuities to ensure lifetime income. Protect against income shortfall risk, sequence of returns risk, systematic risk, and interest rate risk
Cash Value Life Insurance	Yes, explore but compare plans. Youth and good health can buy cheap insurance and rapidly compounding cash	Yes, especially if legacy motivated. Consider insuring sons or daughters while you maintain ownership and control of cash values	Use policy loans for potentially tax advantaged (currently tax free) retirement income. Many life policies also include Long Term Assisted Care Riders.

The IQ Wealth Smarter Bucketing System™ Consumer's Guide To Income Security, At-A-Glance:

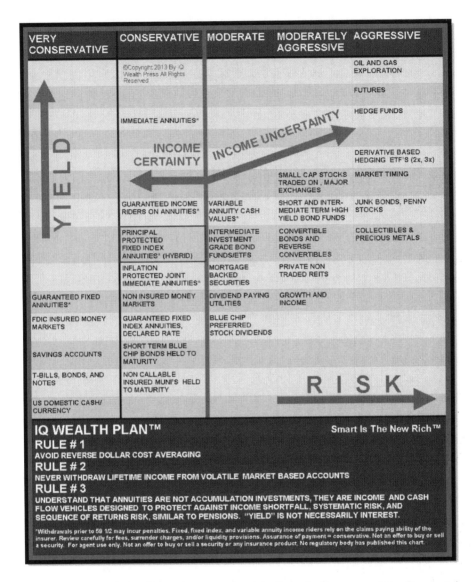

VERY CONSERVATIVE	CONSERVATIVE	MODERATE	MODERATELY AGGRESSIVE	AGGRESSIVE
	©Copyright 2013 By iQ Wealth Press All Rights Reserved			OIL AND GAS EXPLORATION
				FUTURES
				HEDGE FUNDS
	IMMEDIATE ANNUITIES*			
	INCOME CERTAINTY			DERIVATIVE BASED HEDGING ETF'S (2x, 3x)
			SMALL CAP STOCKS TRADED ON , MAJOR EXCHANGES	MARKET TIMING
	GUARANTEED INCOME RIDERS ON ANNUITIES*	VARIABLE ANNUITY CASH VALUES*	SHORT AND INTER-MEDIATE TERM HIGH YIELD BOND FUNDS	JUNK BONDS, PENNY STOCKS
	PRINCIPAL PROTECTED FIXED INDEX ANNUITIES* (HYBRID)	INTERMEDIATE INVESTMENT GRADE BOND FUNDS/ETFS	CONVERTIBLE BONDS AND REVERSE CONVERTIBLES	COLLECTIBLES & PRECIOUS METALS
	INFLATION PROTECTED JOINT IMMEDIATE ANNUITIES*	MORTGAGE BACKED SECURITIES	PRIVATE NON TRADED REITS	
GUARANTEED FIXED ANNUITIES*	NON INSURED MONEY MARKETS	DIVIDEND PAYING UTILITIES	GROWTH AND INCOME	
FDIC INSURED MONEY MARKETS	GUARANTEED FIXED INDEX ANNUITIES, DECLARED RATE	BLUE CHIP PREFERRED STOCK DIVIDENDS		
SAVINGS ACCOUNTS	SHORT TERM BLUE CHIP BONDS HELD TO MATURITY			
T-BILLS, BONDS, AND NOTES	NON CALLABLE INSURED MUNI'S HELD TO MATURITY			
US DOMESTIC CASH/ CURRENCY				

YIELD

INCOME UNCERTAINTY

R I S K

IQ WEALTH PLAN™

Smart Is The New Rich™

RULE # 1
AVOID REVERSE DOLLAR COST AVERAGING

RULE # 2
NEVER WITHDRAW LIFETIME INCOME FROM VOLATILE MARKET BASED ACCOUNTS

RULE # 3
UNDERSTAND THAT ANNUITIES ARE NOT ACCUMULATION INVESTMENTS, THEY ARE INCOME AND CASH FLOW VEHICLES DESIGNED TO PROTECT AGAINST INCOME SHORTFALL, SYSTEMATIC RISK, AND SEQUENCE OF RETURNS RISK, SIMILAR TO PENSIONS. "YIELD" IS NOT NECESSARILY INTEREST.

*Withdrawals prior to 59 1/2 may incur penalties. Fixed, fixed index, and variable annuity income riders rely on the claims paying ability of the insurer. Review carefully for fees, surrender charges, and/or liquidity provisions. Assurance of payment = conservative. Not an offer to buy or sell a security. For agent use only. Not an offer to buy or sell a security or any insurance product. No regulatory body has published this chart.

Securing contractually guaranteed cash flow is the secret to financial peace of mind. Don't let your broker or the media talk you out of an annuity. Get the facts.

Boring But Beautiful—The Annuities Of Old Are A Thing of The Past. Enter the Next Generation.

Efficiency and practicality are boring. They are also reasons why you might choose a hybrid or fuel efficient car. The foundation to your house is also pretty boring. Most of it is underground, so you really don't give it much thought—unless it cracks. Foundations are boring but they are beautiful. The many investors now choosing Hybrid index annuities for all or part of their 401(k) and 403b rollovers are putting themselves in a much more solid position of control, flexibility, and future income. They are focused on building a foundation. Is that not a smart thing to do? Rather than choosing to invest with no floor in progressively risky markets, or placing too much money in an immediate annuity or variable annuity where control is lost and fees are high, more men and women are choosing the Next Generation hybrid index. It is a foundation asset--a safe and practical income generator in an era of great uncertainty. Compare the many income riders available to add even more personal control.

According to studies at Harvard, Stanford, Boston University, The University of Illinois, and the Wharton School of Business, most Americans need an annuity in some form. Much of the research has been done using immediate income annuities. Immediate annuities have their place, but for a 50, 60, or 70 year old, it may still be too early to "annuitize." The Hybrid index annuity preserves the ability to annuitize and even offers a "light" version of annuitizing - the income rider we discussed in **Chapter 14.**

Retirees are on a precipice. Central bank stimulation is smoothing out the bumps for now, but increasing the potential for pain at a later date. Smart retirees are moving to safer financial havens now, before the next major economic downturn. The biggest financial risk retirees face today isn't found in the stock market – it's found in themselves. It is the question of how long they will live – and, therefore, how long their resources will have to last. It is the question of how the financial decisions made today will affect them

15 years from today.

I repeat: **Success Leaves Clues.** You know a successful person when you see one. They're living life and loving life. **Locking in your idea of success while your mind is clear and your assets are intact is the only way you can be certain that you won't screw things up later.** There's no time like the present. Get off your duff.

All of us make mistakes but, at minimum, make sure you know the difference between saving, investing, speculating, and insuring.

Is there a risk that you may outlive your savings? Of course there is. Will the 4 percent "Safe Withdrawal Rule" save you? Of course not. Shift happens, and bear markets chew up money. The only financial asset that can guarantee to pay you a permanent sustained income no matter how long you live is an annuity. Annuities don't cost you; they pay you. And, most important, they never stop paying you.

Is There A Luxury Hybrid In Your Future?

Hybrid cars will come in luxury sports car versions and in ten years could dominate all car purchases. Annuities may take their rightful place in financial planning: a source of safety, security and income that can't be found with bond funds. In a time of growing uncertainties in highly volatile markets being run by algorithms who don't care about you or your retirement dreasms, get an annuity going in your plan. The insurance company is required to care about you. When dreams and hopes of massive accumulation give way to the increasing need for good old fashioned income in higher quantities, an annuity strategy may offer some or all of the following:

- **S**pecific income at specific times in specific amounts
- **M**easurable results, mathematically determined
- **A**ttainable levels of income at higher rates of cash flow than quality bonds
- **R**eliable. Income guarantees are backed by measured reserves

- Timely control of your income capital in retirement, no surprises
- Protection from market declines--a financial floor under your money
- No front end fees, no annual management fees, no subaccount fees
- 100% of your money goes to work right away
- Worry free inflation protection from a growing income base
- Income efficient—uses fewer dollars to result in more income
- Mortality credit--The older you get, the more income you can receive
- Can replace the pension you never had
- Recession resistant—fixed annuities have endured wars and recessions
- Safety and security for your principal, similar to holding bonds Penalty free withdrawals of up to 10 percent annually—ample liquidity
- Surrender charges that decline over time, then disappear. No surrender charges on allowable partial withdrawals.
- A minimum of fees (the only actual fees deducted are optional riders)
- A steadily growing, ever increasing pension-like income on demand
- Flexibility in timing of income
- Specificity in amount of income
- Enhanced income benefits available through income riders, often at superior payouts to variable annuity riders
- Surrender charges waived upon death
- Additional long term care supplementation on some annuities
- Inflation protection and enhanced death benefit protection without health exam.

Critics of hybrid annuities play the same eight-track cassette tape, hopelessly lost in 1995. They will say: "What about the 'unlimited upside' of the stock market you are missing out on?" I can only say, "what about the unlimited downside" at the risk of sounding old school. But let's drill deeper. Few credible market analysts would say we are on the verge of a record breaking upward thrust in markets. Healthy stock markets are built on strong economies, the kind that employ 95% of people seeking work and can provide careers, not just jobs for young people. Yes, a Fed induced cyclical bull market can happen any time. So can regression to the mean.

Far from being a doom-and-gloomer, I know there is always a place for optimism and a well thought out equity growth strategy. In fact, I build institutional management into my financial plans. For the growth bucket, I prefer a carefully selected dividend reinvestment strategy. At IQ Wealth Management, we oversea the Black Diamond Dividend portfolio. It requires a minimum of ten consecutive years of dividend growth (the company must raise its dividend every year to remain in the portfolio.) There are 7 other criteria as well. You find out more at www.BlackDiamondDividend.com

Our financial bucketing system includes four buckets:

1) **Bucket One:** cash/liquidity. This is where money markets and bank accounts are assets of choice

2) **Bucket Two:** fixed income and preservation. This is where annuities are the asset of choice.;

3) **Bucket Three:** long term growth. This is where a dividend reinvestment strategy centered around high quality, profitable companies can make sense. Dividend growth stocks pay you constantly to own them, and give you a raise every year.

4) **Bucket Four:** insured outcomes. This is where the focus is on

estate planning and long term care needs, and my be optional. Everyone is different and all of us have different legacy motives. Some of us want to leave a lot to the next generation, some not so much, and some want their last check to bounce (to the IRS of course!)

All of the buckets are important. Each helps the other. The annuity bucket helps you in this way: Because it will generate more income using up less of your money, you have more money to invest for growth in Bucket 3. Logical. Math-based. In fact,

One day, *not* owning an annuity in some form, may qualify you for membership in the "Flat Earth Society".

Retirement tip from a Retirement Coach:

Hope is not a strategy. Stop obsessing about missing out on another 10% of upside growth, while exposing yourself to a 30% loss. You are retiring, already retired, or are crossing the 50-yard line, headed for the end zone! Score. Don't blow it. You shouldn't have to ask permission from your stock broker to move money to safety.

If control of your money is important to you, then at least 25 percent of your money should be safely growing and protected by the benefits of a hybrid index annuity from a solid carrier. It's common sense. If falls under the heading of "No one ever went broke taking a profit." No one ever went broke taking a 5% to 7% income, guaranteed for life, either.

How Much Money Do You Need To Retire, *Really*?

A popular book on retirement recently asked, "What's your Number?" The question refers to the amount of money you will need to retire, and stay retired, while paying yourself an income forever. According to documented academic and institutional studies, compiled by university PhDs, actuaries, and CPA firms, **you're going to need more money than you think.** Historic low interest rates, shaky stock markets, and longer lifespans are turning retirement planning upside down. The old 4 percent safe withdrawal rate is failing many retirees, at a time when they can't afford to go backwards with their money. If 95 turns out to be the new 86, A 55 year old woman needs to make sure the money she depends on for survival will be not only remain intact, but still be paying out income 40 years from now. Murphy's Law says if you plan for 95 and spend your last dollar, you'll live to 96.

Seven years ago, retiring Americans' biggest fear was "dying," according to studies by Cerulli Associates, the Boston-based research firm. Today, after two "once in a lifetime" market declines, and with bank interest rates hovering near zero, American's greatest fear has become running out of money.

The nonpartisan Employee Benefit Research Institute revealed that 64 percent of Americans in the lowest income levels will run out of money in retirement inside of 10 years. The most alarming finding, however, was that 13 percent of Americans in the highest income bracket will run out of money after only 20 to 21 years in the typical stock and bond portfolio; and 90 percent of higher earners without a pension or annuity are at risk of living completely on Social Security in their lifetimes. Clearly, a financial strategy that addresses longevity risk, not just market risk, is needed.

Chances are, you are underestimating your needs for future income while obsessing over financial growth.

It's time to start obsessing over income. Traditional investments may work in traditional times, but there's nothing traditional about today. You need income now, and you will need it until your dying day.

With a traditional plan, when you run out of money, you're out of income. Income is the fuel your retirement will run on.

Are you running on sustainable fuel? Or fossil fuel? Dump that gas guzzler for a luxury hybrid! Trade in some of that market-reliant income for mathematically determined and carefully-planned income. Make sure you don't run out of money before you run out of time.

Pure cash used to be a safe haven. But cash is no longer a risk-free return – it's a *return-free risk*. In fact, stationary cash is no longer "king." Cash *flow*, is king. Smart is the new rich. Permanent cash flow allows you to satisfy your long-held ambitions, rather than just covering your nagging obligations. "Getting by" is no fun and is not what you've worked for. Life is a journey – destination, unknown. Face it, you wouldn't have it any other way.

Hemingway said, *"It is good to have an end to journey toward; but it is the journey that matters, in the end."* He owned an annuity known as book royalties, so he had time on his hands to come up with gems like that. You can too, with a little planning. Life is a journey, but it takes money to get there.

> **"Not I, nor anyone else can travel that road for you.**
> **You must travel it by yourself. It is not far.**
> **It is within reach. Perhaps you have been on it since you were born,**
> **and did not know.**
> **Perhaps it is everywhere – on water and land."**
> -*Walt Whitman*

I'm with Walt on this one. This is a beautiful life, your one last moment to shine. "you're never ever too old, you've never been too bad, it's never too late, and you're never too sick to start from scratch once again." True.

But cruise ships and RVs cost money.

Your journey begins today. I hope to see you out there,

living life to the fullest, with no money worries,

no matter what.

Give me a two-finger salute as you drive by or a tip of the cap as you sail past. I'll be loving it.

As your retirement coach,

I'll leave you with this parting advice:

> **Avoid D.U.M.B. mistakes,**
>
> **Be S.M.A.R.T. with your money,**
>
> **Don't be "All Thumbs,"**
>
> **And don't forget AFORI.**
>
> **I wish you all success, excellent L.U.C.K. and hey...**
>
> **A little C.H.E.A.T.(ing)**
>
> **may not hurt either...**

Be safe, ciao .

DISCLAIMER

The information contained in this document has not been approved or disapproved by any insurance department, department of securities, or regulatory body. All information contained herein represents the opinion of the author only. It should not become the sole basis for any financial decisions and no actions should ever be taken without the careful assistance of a financial professional, licensed in the area of study, after a thorough personal review. While the author has been careful to utilize information from sources deemed reliable and from recognized papers in the mainstream of academic research, the reader accepts the responsibility of verifying all information and sources prior to taking any financial actions based on any information contained herein. No legal, investment, or tax advice is being offered, and there is no offer to buy or sell a security nor any specific insurance product. No reference resources endorse or recommend any investment ideas, investments, annuities, or products.

Not all annuity or investment products are suitable for all investors or consumers. Variable annuities are sold by prospectus. Nothing in this publication is an offer to buy or sell a security or a promotion of any variable annuity product. Past performance should never be relied upon to predict future results. Fixed and fixed index annuities are insurance based products issued by life insurance companies regulated in each state, and all guarantees rely on the claims paying ability of the issuing insurer. While most annuities charge no upfront fee, there can be a substantial penalty for early withdrawal. See your annuity contract: Surrender charge schedules typically range from five to ten years, however some may last as long as fifteen years. Withdrawals prior to age 59 ½ may incur tax penalties not imposed by the insurance companies. Annuities are intended as long term retirement vehicles, are not bank deposits, and are not FDIC insured. Examine your annuity to determine when or how your annuity could lose value. See your contract for liquidity provisions and to learn what date all surrender charges may no longer apply. Generally, surrender charges are waived upon death of the annuitant, but this can very. Examine your annuity for details. Be clear on all details prior to commitment. Meet with a qualified professional, with proper licensing. No tax, legal, or investment advice is offered herein.

REFERENCES

Research and Reference guide (partial list), and recommended reading:

Jeffrey R. Brown, *The New Retirement Challenge, Americans for Secure Retirement* (September, 2004). Access location:
http://www.paycheckforlife.org/uploads/ASR_whitepapers.pdf

David F. Babbel and Craig B. Merrill, *Rational Decumulation*, Wharton Financial Institutions Center (May, 2007). Access location:
http://fic.wharton.upenn.edu/fic/papers/06/p0614.htm

Live Q&A Session with Secretary Solis (December 7, 2009). It can be accessed here:
http://www.dol.gov/regulations/chat-solis.htm

Strategies for Coping After Retiring Into a Bear Market, T. Rowe Price Research (April, 2008). Access location: http://www.troweprice.com/gcFiles/pdf/2A37-RetiringBearMarket.pdf?scn=Articles&src=Media_Near_or_In_Retirement&t=lgcy

Eleanor Laise, *Odds-On Imperfection: Monte Carlo Simulation*, *The Wall Street Journal* (May 2, 2009). It can be accessed here:
http://online.wsj.com/article/SB124121875397178921.html SSA actuarial tables accessible here: http://www.ssa.gov/OACT/STATS/table4c6.html

2010, 2011, 2012 Quantitative Analysis of Investor Behavior, Dalbar, Inc. www.Dalbar.com

The "new math" of the distribution phase, American Funds Research (Winter, 2007). It can be accessed here:
http://www.oakadvisors.com/files/American_funds_new_math.pdf

Retirement vulnerability of new retirees: The likelihood of outliving their assets, by Ernst & Young for Americans for Secure Retirement (July, 2008). It can be accessed here: http://www.paycheckforlife.org/uploads/2008_E_Y_RRA.pdf

The Budget and Economic Outlook: Fiscal Years 2009 to 2019, Congressional Budget Office (January, 2009). It can be accessed here:
http://www.cbo.gov/ftpdocs/99xx/doc9957/01-07-Outlook.pdf

The Budget and Economic Outlook: Fiscal Years 2010 to 2020, Congressional Budget Office (January, 2010). It can be accessed here:
http://www.cbo.gov/ftpdocs/108xx/doc10871/01-26-Outlook.pdf

The Decline in Eligible Traditional Pension Plan Participants, Employee Benefit Research Institute (February 1, 2007). It can be accessed here: http://www.ebri.org/pdf/publications/facts/fastfacts/fastfact020107.pdf;

Retirement Trends in the United States Over the Past Quarter-Century, Employee Benefit Research Institute (June, 2007). It can be accessed here: http://www.ebri.org/pdf/campaign/Cmpg08_R_2-a.pdf;

A Safer Safe Withdrawal Rate Using Various Return Distributions by Manoj Athavale, Ph.D., and Joseph M. Goebel, Ph.D. http://www.fpanet.org/journal/CurrentIssue/TableofContents/ASaferSafeWithdra walRateUsingVariousDistributions/

Robert J. Shiller, *Irrational Exuberance* (Princeton University Press, 2005).

David F. Babbel and Craig B. Merrill, *Investing your Lump Sum at Retirement, Wharton Financial Institutions Center* (August 14, 2007). It can be accessed here: http://fic.wharton.upenn.edu/fic/Policy%20page/WhartonEssay18.pdf

Jeff, P. Opdyke, *The Case for 'Income Annuities", The Wall Street Journal* (August 8.2007). http://online.wsj.com/article/SB118652918652491009.html

Analytical Perspectives: Budget of the United States, Fiscal Year 2010, Office of Management and Budget (February 26, 2009). It can be accessed here: http://www.gpoaccess.gov/usbudget/fy10/pdf/spec.pdf

David F. Babbel, *Lifetime Income for Women: A Financial Economist's Perspective,* Wharton Financial Institutions Center (August 12, 2008). It can be accessed here: http://fic.wharton.upenn.edu/fic/Policy%20page/Lifetime%20Income%20for%20 Women%206.9.09.pdf

12 *The 2009 Retirement Confidence Survey*, Employee Benefit Research Institute (April, 2009). It can be accessed here: http://www.ebri.org/publications/ib/index.cfm?fa=ibdisp&content_id=4226

Jeffrey R. Brown, *The New Retirement Challenge, Americans for Secure Retirement* (September, 2004). http://www.paycheckforlife.org/uploads/ASR_whitepapers.pdf

David F. Babbel and Craig B. Merrill, *Rational Decumulation*, Wharton Financial Institutions Center (May, 2007). It can be accessed here: http://fic.wharton.upenn.edu/fic/papers/06/p0614.htm

Live Q&A Session with Secretary Solis (December 7, 2009). It can be accessed here: http://www.dol.gov/regulations/chat-solis.htm

Strategies for Coping After Retiring Into a Bear Market, T. Rowe Price Research (April, 2008). It can be accessed here: http://www.troweprice.com/gcFiles/pdf/2A37-RetiringBearMarket.pdf?scn=Articles&src=Media_Near_or_In_Retirement&t=lgcy

Eleanor Laise, *Odds-On Imperfection: Monte Carlo Simulation, The Wall Street Journal* (May 2, 2009). Access location: http://online.wsj.com/article/SB124121875397178921.html

SSA actuarial tables: http://www.ssa.gov/OACT/STATS/table4c6.html

Half of U.S. Babies Living Today May Reach 100, Atlanta Journal-Constitution (October 2, 2009).: http://www.ajc.com/health/content/shared-auto/healthnews/age-/631574.htmlD

"Annuities and Retirement Well-being," 2004, Chapter 14 in Pension Design and Structure: *New Lessons from Behavioral Finance*, Olivia S. Mitchell and Stephen P. Utkus (eds), ISBN 0-19-927339-1. Oxford: Oxford University Press. Also referenced at: http://www.aacg.com/extras/StanPanis_AACG.pdf

An International Perspective on Safe Withdrawal Rates: The Demise of the 4 Percent Rule? by Wade D. Pfau, Ph.D. http://www.fpanet.org/journal/CurrentIssue/TableofContents/AnInternationalPerspectiveonSafeWithdrawalRates/

Dow Jones Historical Trends http://www.risadvisory.com/images/uploads/Rydex_Historical_trends.pdf

National Association of Insurance Commissioners Guiide To Fixed Annuities http://www.piam.com/Financial_Services/NAIC_BGAnnuities09.pdf